1971

ANTHONY COMSTOCK

A Da Capo Press Reprint Series

CIVIL LIBERTIES IN AMERICAN HISTORY

GENERAL EDITOR: LEONARD W. LEVY

Claremont Graduate School

ANTHONY COMSTOCK

His Career of Cruelty and Crime

By D. R. M. Bennett

DA CAPO PRESS • NEW YORK • 1971

A Da Capo Press Reprint Edition

This Da Capo Press edition of
Anthony Comstock
is an unabridged republication of the
first edition published in New York in 1878.

Library of Congress Catalog Card Number 73-121102

SBN 306-71968-1

Published by Da Capo Press
A Division of Plenum Publishing Corporation
227 West 17th Street
New York, N. Y. 10011

ANTHONY COMSTOCK

Anthony Comstock

HIS

Career of Cruelty and Crime

A CHAPTER FROM

'The Champions of the Church"

BY D. M. BENNETT.

Price Twenty-Five Cents.

NEW YORK:
D. M. BENNETT,
LIBERAL AND SCIENTIFIC PUBLISHING HOUSE,
SCIENCE HALL, 141 EIGHTH STREET.
1878.

ANTHONY COMSTOCK.

THIS compilation of Christian Champions—those who in the name of morality and the Christian religion have persecuted and annoyed others—would be incomplete without a reasonable notice of the character who heads this sketch. It would be doing himself and the public serious injustice not to place him side by side with those unworthy compeers of his who have abused the arbitrary power which for a time was placed in their hands. In every instance these persecutors who in the past have been so ready to ruthlessly deprive of liberty, happiness, and life their unfortunate victims, who did not subscribe to the doctrines enjoined by the ruling powers, have done so in the name of the religion of Jesus and under the auspices of the highest system of morality said to be known to man.

Comstock has evinced the same energy, the same cruelty the same intolerance, the same hardness of heart, and the same unyielding persistence in harassing and hunting down those who presumed to differ from the orthodox standard of religious thought—and have dared to be independent in matters of theology, medicine, and the literature pertaining to them—that have marked the envenomed persecutors of the past centuries. It is the time and the advance that has been made in civilization that have made the difference. This man has evinced the disposition of hatred and cruelty that a few centuries ago would have made a first-class Torquemada, Calvin, Alva, Charles IX., or Matthew Hopkins. Could he have the power he craves and the requisite opportunity, it is not to be supposed he would be far behind those notorious characters in the work of desolation, cruelty, and bitter persecution which they showed themselves so capable of performing. He evidently engages in his work of persecution with the same degree of zeal and pleasure that marked the conduct of the Christian torturers and assassins alluded to. It is seriously doubted whether the Church has ever had a cruel zealot in its employ who has labored with more resolution and zest than this active agent of the Young Men's Christian Association.

It is not to be denied that those bloody persecutors, commissioned by the Church to torture and slay the hapless victims who fell in their way, each possessed some good qualities and that among the heartless acts they performed, some were commendable. So it is with Anthony Comstock; he has done some good; and far is it from the writer of these pages to deny him any of the good he has performed, though the means by which he reaches his ends, and by which he brings the unfortunate to punishment, are not such as good men can approve. Among a certain class of vile publishers he has accomplished a reform that must be placed to his credit, but the system of falsehood, subterfuge, and decoy-letters that he has employed to entrap his victims and inveigle them into the commission of an offense against the laws is utterly to be condemned.

The want of discrimination which he has evinced between those who were really guilty of issuing vile publications—whose only object was to inflame the baser passions—and those who published and sold books for the purpose of educating and improving mankind, has been a serious defect with this man. While he has suppressed much that is vile, he has, to a much larger extent, infringed upon the dearest rights of the individual, thus bringing obloquy and disgrace upon those who had a good object in view. And upon those who, in a limited degree, were in fault, he has been severe and relentless to a criminal extent. He has evinced far too much pleasure in bringing his fellow-beings into the deepest sorrow and grief; and under the name of arresting publishers of, and dealers in, obscene literature, he has caused the arraignment of numerous persons who had not the slightest intention of violating the rules of propriety and morality. Could he have expended his zeal and energy only upon those who deserved punishment, and have brought them under the rule of the law by fair and honorable means, his record would stand far better than it does to-day.

In that case he would not have been compelled to make the humiliating confession which he made in a public meeting of clergymen and others in Boston, May 30, 1878, where he was endeavoring to organize a branch, auxiliary "Society for the Suppression of Vice," the parent society of which is of Comstock's origination, and located in New York. While Comstock was addressing the meeting, the Rev. Jesse H. Jones (Congregationalist) arose, and expressed a wish to ask Mr. Comstock a few questions. He was permitted to ask three, when a disposition was manifested that the interrogatories be not continued. The questions propounded were as follow: 1. "Did you, Mr. Comstock, ever use decoy letters and false signatures? 2. Did you ever sign a woman's name to such decoy letters? 3. Did you ever try to make persons sell you forbidden wares, and then, when you had succeeded, use the evidence thus obtained to convict them?" To each of these questions Comstock answered, "Yes, I have done it," whereupon Mr. Jones, with firmness of manner, asserted that "Mr. Comstock had been guilty of what would be considered disgraceful in a Boston policeman." It is unfortunate for the reputation of Mr. Comstock, and the society which sustains him, and in whose name he works, that the most of his business, and the larger share of his victims and arrests have been brought about by these agencies. He has simply acted the part of a despicable spy and detective. Falsehood, deception, traps, and pitfalls for the unwary have been the agencies he has employed in the prosecution of his nefarious business. It is confidently asserted that he has written thousands upon thousands of decoy letters, bearing fictitious signatures of both men and women, and written for the purpose of inducing unsuspecting persons to commit an offense against the law and to be guilty of a crime which they would not otherwise have thought of committing. It must be admitted by all honorable men that this is a contemptible course to be pursued by a society of moral, high-minded men, which was organized in the name of morality and the Christian religion. It is a question for moralists to decide whether, when a cause or a system has to be sustained by such a dishonorable course of conduct, it would not be better that the society disband and its agent resort to a more honorable means of obtaining a livelihood.

Anthony Comstock is a native of New Canaan, Conn., where he was born March 9, 1844, and where he resided through childhood and youth. It is unnecessary to inquire into the details of his early life. There have been worse boys as well as many far better than he was. When quite a young man, and during the war of the Rebellion, he obtained a position as sutler's clerk in one of the Connecticut regiments, which he held for a while, but for sufficient reasons was discharged. Subsequently, about the years 1871 and 1872, he was in the employ of the dry-goods house of Cochran & McLean, 464 Broadway, New York, where he served in the capacity of traveling salesman; but in due time the firm saw fit to dispense with his services.

It was while connected with this dry goods house that Comstock seems to have conceived the brilliant idea of waging a warfare upon the publishers and venders of obscene literature, as well as all who dared to deviate from the rule prescribed by his saintly societies. Being a member of the Young Men's Christian Association, he not only acted under their auspices to a certain extent, but he originated a new organization, called "The New York Society for the Suppression of Vice," or rather, perfected an organization that had previously been begun. It was modeled and named after a similar society in London, which made it its business to hunt down and prosecute those who do not think and act according to the orthodox standard, and which in 1877 prosecuted Mr. Charles Bradlaugh and Mrs. Annie Besant for publishing Dr. Charles Knowlton's "Fruits of Philosophy," a work of merit which has been sold for forty years in that country and in this; and in the spring of 1878 prosecuted and convicted Edward Truelove, an old Freethought publisher eighty-six years of age, and secured a sentence of four months' imprisonment and a fine of fifty pounds sterling. His offense was selling Robert Dale Owen's "Moral Physiology," a work of decided value which has been sold in England and in the United States for more than a generation.

The London Society for the Suppression of Vice was founded three-fourths of a century earlier than its namesake of New York, and was conducted by the same system of espionage, decoying, and informing that has characterized its more modern namesake; and so learned and good a man as Sydney Smith entertained a very indifferent opinion as to the character of the men composing it. He says: "It is hardly possible that a society for the suppression of vice can ever be kept within the bounds of good sense and moderation. If there are many members who have really become so from a feeling of duty, there will necessarily be some who enter the society to hide a bad character, and others whose object it is to recommend themselves to their betters by a sedulous and bustling inquisition into the immoralities of the public. The loudest and noisiest suppressors will always carry it against the more prudent part of·the community; the most violent will be considered as the most moral; and those who see the absurdity will, from the fear of being thought to encourage vice, be reluctant to oppose it. . . . Beginning with the best intentions in the world, such societies must, in all probability, degenerate into a receptacle for every species of tittle-tattle, impertinence, and malice. Men whose trade is rat-catching, love to catch rats; the bug-destroyer seizes on his bug with delight; and the suppressor is gratified by finding his vice. The last soon becomes a mere tradesman like the others; none of them moralize, or lament that their respective evils should exist in the world. The public feeling is swallowed up in the pursuit of a daily occupation, and in the display of a technical skill."

As to Sydney Smith's views of the means and the kind of agents which the society employed to secure its victims and to make its arrests, he expressed himself as follows: " An informer, whether paid by the week, like the agents of this society, or by the crime, as in common cases, is in general a man of a very indifferent character. So much fraud and deception are necessary for carrying on his trade—it is so odious to his fellow-subjects—that *no man of respectability will ever undertake it.* It is evidently impossible to make such a character otherwise than odious. A man who receives weekly pay for prying into the transgressions of mankind, and bringing them to consequent punishment, will always be hated by mankind, and the office must fall to the lot of some man of desperate fortunes and ambiguous character. If it be lawful for respectable men to combine for the purpose of turning informers, it is lawful for the lowest and most despicable race of informers to do the same thing; and then it is quite clear that every species of wickedness and extortion would be the consequence."

Every candid person must acknowledge the correctness and force of these remarks. An honorable, good man will never willingly accept the office of a spy and informer to lie in wait and watch for the errors and weaknesses of his fellow-beings and then, by decoying them on and entrapping them, use their simplicity or their confidence to throw them into prison and effect their utter ruin.

The New York Society for the Suppression of Vice was incorporated by the Legislature of New York, May 16, 1873, chiefly through the efforts of Anthony Comstock, its secretary and active agent, and the Young Men's Christian Association. He also procured the enactment by the United States Congress, and by the Legislature of New York State of a series of acts, which were placed in both the national and State statute books, and which are believed by many to be subversive of the very principles of American liberty and destructive to individual rights guaranteed by the Constitution of our country. Of the some half dozen of these Comstock acts, which by his urgent efforts have become parts of the laws of our land, two sections will here be given as specimens of all:

SEC. 3893. No obscene, lewd, or lascivious book, pamphlet, picture, paper, print, or other publication of an indecent character, or any article or thing designed or intended for the prevention of conception or procuring of abortion, nor any article or thing intended or adapted for any indecent or immoral use or nature, nor any written or printed card, circular, book, pamphlet, advertisement, or notice of any kind giving information, directly or indirectly, where or how, or of whom, or by what means either of the things before mentioned may be obtained or made, nor any letter upon the envelope of which, or postal card upon which indecent or scurrilous epithets may be written or printed, shall be carried in the mail; and any person who shall knowingly deposit, or cause to be deposited, for mailing or delivery, any of the herein before-mentioned articles or things, or any notice or paper containing any advertisement relating to the aforesaid articles or things; and any person who, in pursuance of any plan or scheme for disposing of any of the herein before-mentioned articles or things, shall take or cause to be taken, from the mail any such letter or package, shall be deemed guilty of a misdemeanor, and shall, for every offense, be fined not less than one hundred dollars, nor more than five thousand dollars, or imprisoned at hard labor not less than one year, nor more than ten years, or both.

SEC. 5389. Every person who, within the District of Columbia, or any of the Territories of the United States, or other place within the exclusive jurisdiction of the United States, sells, or lends, or gives away, or in any manner exhibits or offers to sell, or to lend, or to give away, or in any manner to exhibit, or otherwise publishes or offers to publish in any manner, or has in his possession, for any such purpose, any obscene book, pamphlet, paper, writing, advertisement, circular, print, picture, drawing, or other representation, figure, or image on or of paper or other material, or any cast, instrument, or other article of an immoral nature, or any drug or medicine, or any article whatever, for the prevention of conception, or for causing unlawful abortion, or who advertises the same for sale, or writes or prints, or causes to be written or printed, any card, circular, book, pamphlet, advertisement, or notice of any kind, stating when, where, how, or of whom, or by what means, any of the articles in this section hereinbefore mentioned can be procured or obtained; or manufactures, draws, or prints, or in anywise makes any of such articles, shall be imprisoned at hard labor in the penitentiary for not less than six months, nor more than five years for each offense, or fined not less than one hundred dollars, nor more than two thousand dollars, with costs of court.

While there are commendable features in these laws it must be confessed that the foregoing sections are excessively severe, besides being indefinite. When such heavy penalties are imposed, the offenses for which they are prescribed should be clearly marked out. If obscenity, indecency, and immor-

ality are crimes to be punished by fines of $5,000 and imprison-
ment at hard labor for ten years, they should at least be clearly
defined, so that every person can know what 'the law considers
immoral, what indecent, and what obscene.

A learned jurist has said that " no legislative body in making laws should use language that has to be defined and construed by others. Every crime should be so clearly defined
that there can be no mistaking it. Murder, homicide, arson,
larceny, burglary, forgery, and so forth, are so defined that
they cannot be misunderstood. It is not so with obscenity ;
the term is left to be construed by judges, lawyers, juries, and
whoever chooses to decide what *is* obscene and what is *not.*
If obscenity is a crime punishable by fine and imprisonment,
it at least ought to be correctly described so that it may be
known in what it consists, and so that an accused person
shall not be at the mercy of a man or a number of men who
construe what is obscene, what is indecent and immoral, by
their own particular opinion or notion of morality and immorality. What is obscene to one man may be as pure as the
mountain snow to another, and one man should not be empowered to decide for other men."

To procure the enactment of the foregoing laws, Comstock
made frequent journeys to Washington, and ' he carried with
him, it is said, a satchel full of lewd, filthy books, pictures,
and devices which he spread out before congressmen and
which he induced them to believe were being sent through
the mail by scores of tons to the youth of the country
and to the young school children at seminaries, boarding-
schools, and so forth. After the law-makers had been
regaled with a view of these unclean curiosities, they seemed
to be prepared to vote, Aye, on almost any kind of laws for
which their vote might be solicited. It is to be regretted that
they could not have displayed better judgment than to
destroy the very principles of American Liberty and Individual Freedom for the sake of protecting school children from
the imaginary belief that improper mail matter was sent them.
If it is true that such mail matter is sent them, how easy

it would be to obviate it by having it inspected by teachers or guardians before passing it over to the children. This could be readily done without violating the Constitution of our country or crushing the rights of the entire people.

The time and mode by which these laws were enacted were extremely discreditable to American legislation. The final passage took place in the closing hours of the Forty-second Congress, on the third of March, 1873, when within a few hours, and when the house was in the wildest state of confusion, and numbers of the members were under the influence of ardent spirits, some two hundred and sixty acts were hurried through without inquiry or consideration. In many instances even the titles of the bills voted upon were unknown to members.

The signing by President Grant was performed in the same hurried, reckless manner. Hundreds of laws were thus signed by him without the slightest examination on his part and as rapidly as, one after another, they could be handed him by an attendant. And thus were placed upon our statute books a set of laws that should never have appeared there in the way they do. The personal wrongs that have been inflicted under them have not been few nor trivial.

A very similar set of laws were, by the personal exertions of Mr. Comstock, and by a similar style of tactics, passed by the Legislature at Albany and became a part of the laws of the State of New York, and combined with the United States laws just referred to, they have proved an engine of oppression to many individuals who under them have been suddenly brought to the deepest grief.

It will probably not be out of place to briefly narrate some of the cases which Mr. Comstock has mercilessly prosecuted under the laws which he procured to be enacted, as well as to show the true character of the man when he is able to bring unfortunate persons under the weight of his power. Attention is called to the means employed by him in securing his victims and the amount of mercy evinced towards them when brought under his ban.

1. Case of Charles Mackey, of New York, who was engaged in publishing a popular weekly story paper and in selling a miscellaneous variety of books, and who was arrested by Comstock in 1872 or '73. Mackey issued a catalogue of his books which he sent out to various parts of the country. Comstock sent to him for certain books, by mail, upon which, with the circular, he caused Mackey's arrest. There were no obscene books among Mackey's stock, though some of the titles on the catalogue were somewhat suggestive, as " Ovid's Art of Love," " Prostitution in Paris," etc. The case was tried before Judge Benedict of the U. S. Circuit Court. Comstock was the only witness. He testified that he had not received any obscene book from Mackey, and that he did not know of anything obscene that Mackey had in his possession save his catalogue. Mackey's lawyer asked the privilege to show to the jury that none of the books named in the catalogue were of an obscene character. This the judge would not permit, holding that the titles were obscene whether the books were or not. He charged the jury accordingly, whereupon a verdict of guilty was brought in, and Mackey was sentenced to one year's imprisonment besides a fine of $500. It was a heavy blow to Mr. Mackey. Previous to the arrest he stood high in the community and was doing a flourishing business. He was worth some $40,000, but the conviction, trial, and sentence nearly ruined him. His paper expired, his book trade went down, his reputation was blasted, his friends forsook him, and all because Anthony Comstock, Judge Benedict, and the jury did not approve of the title of the books upon his catalogue. It was a decided case of legal persecution and oppression.

On the day Mackey was taken from the prison to be sentenced, Comstock showed the natural meanness of his character by requesting that handcuffs be placed on Mackey, when he was remanded to prison, the same as upon the thieves and other felons. The suggestion was acted upon, and Mackey, who had stood so fairly in the city, was handcuffed to a convicted thief and thus marched through the streets. Com stock placed himself close by where the prisoners passed, and chuckled and grinned at Mackey as though he enjoyed absolute pleasure in a fellow-being's ignominy and disgrace.

2. CASE OF JAMES SULLIVAN.—This gentleman was a dealer in books and light literature at 113 Fulton street. Comstock, as protector of the morals of the public, visited Sullivan's establishment, and, pulling out three dollars from his pocket and laying them on the counter, said, " I want a copy of 'The Lustful Turk.'" Sullivan replied, " I do not keep that kind of books. You see what stock I have. I will be glad to sell you three dollars' worth of such as I have, but I have none of the kind you call for." Comstock replied that he wished a copy specially of " The Lustful Turk," as he wished to send it to a friend in the country. Sullivan again assured him that he had nothing of the kind. Comstock put his money in his pocket and took his leave.

In February, 1873, Comstock caused the arrested of Sullivan and took him before a United States commissioner for sending information through the mails as to where improper books could be obtained. The Grand Jury, upon Comstock's evidence, found a bill ; and at the trial in the January following, before Judge Benedict, upon Comstock's evidence, a verdict of guilty was easily obtained. Comstock swore that in March, 1872, he had sent a letter from Norwich, or Norwalk, Conn., in the name of Jerry Baxter, to Sullivan, asking for a circular of fancy literature, and that in return he had obtained a list of books of various kinds ; but the list had no name or address upon it to show that it came from Sullivan. Judge Benedict, however, instructed the jury that the reception by Comstock of that circular and envelope, which he had carried in his pocket eleven months before he brought suit, was *prima facie* evidence of Sullivan's guilt. Upon this remarkable ruling, and upon Comstock's uncorroborated testimony, Sullivan was found guilty, and Benedict sentenced him to one year's imprisonment and a fine of $500. Sullivan is ready to take a solemn oath that he never sent the circular ; that the writing on the envelope was not his at all, and that Comstock perjured himself two or three times in giving evidence against him.   But his business was broken up, he was made wretched, and disgraced for life, because Comstock swore that he had received under a fictitious name a catalogue without name or address !   Is this the ultimate of American liberty ?

3. CASE OF LEANDER FOX & SON.—These gentlemen kept a bookstore on Canal street, near West Broadway.   They had been in business many years, and bore a first-class reputation. Mr. Fox, the elder, was advanced in years, and was probably as favorably known, so far as his acquaintance extended, as any man in the city.   He had maintained an unblemished character.   He had, of course, seen his share of the troubles and vicissitudes of life, but it was reserved for Anthony Comstock to bring this gray-haired old man to sorrow, to prison, and disgrace, and to this end he worked assiduously for several years.   During all this time he called repeatedly at the store of Fox & Son and inquired for various obscene and indecent books.   Mr. Fox invariably told the gentleman that he kept nothing of the kind, and never had.

Failing in finding anything there of the sort he is so fond of inquiring after, he resorted to his favorite expedient of writing a decoy letter in a false name and ordering a copy of a work upon which he could arrest him.   He accordingly ordered a copy, to be sent by mail, of Dr. Ashton's " Book of Nature and Marriage Guide " (published and copyrighted by Benjamin T. Day), a work which had been sold regularly for twenty years and by nearly every dealer in the city.   Upon receipt of the order, young Mr. Fox, not having a copy on hand, went out and bought a copy from the trade, and mailed it.   The elder Mr. Fox did not see the order or the book. Comstock was doubtless filled with joy as his eyes fell upon the work thus received, and, " Now," thought he, " I have the game within my grasp that I have been lying in wait for so long."   He lost little time in causing the arrest of father and son for being caught in the trap he had so skillfully set for them, and he had the extreme humanity to cause them to be arrested late on Saturday afternoon in a snow-storm, that they might be unable at that late hour to procure bail, and thus have the ignominy of lying in prison over Sunday. This was a favorite game of Comstock's, and he has played it upon many occasions. But Mr. Fox, being so well known, was able to procure bail, and to evade the punishment that Comstock had so cunningly planned for him.

Messrs. Fox & Son employed the distinguished attorney, William A. Beach, to defend them, but Comstock managed to have the case brought on while Mr. Beach was at Albany, and they were thus placed at great disadvantage, and were unable even to procure such witnesses as they should have had. Under the circumstances, it was very little trouble for Comstock to swear both father and son into prison.

The jury, such as they know how to get up in the United States District Court, found them guilty, and sentenced them to prison for a year.

Think for a moment of the sad havoc such an event must have caused in their business, the sorrow and agony it must have created in their families. Think of the grief of the wife of the old gentleman, who had sojourned with him through life's trials, to have him cruelly torn from her by such a malicious hand and thrown into prison upon the disgraceful charge of dealing in obscene literature and sending it through the mails.

Fortunately for Mr. Fox, he had a warm friend in Thurlow Weed, who, as soon as he learned that his friends Fox & Son were in prison for selling a book of which many thousands had been previously sold, and having great influence with President Grant, succeeded in having both father and son pardoned out. " Kissing goes by favor," and when a man is in prison it is a lucky thing to have a friend who has influence at court, but when a poor man, without friends, gets into prison, no matter how unjust the conviction may be, he would have to serve his time out, though death might be his fate before it was over. As it was, Fox and his son had to lie several months in durance, and at a time, too, when another son was on his dying bed without the presence and care of his father. Should the Fox family entertain the warmest affection for Anthony Comstock, who is such a special favorite with the Y. M. C. A. and the S. F. S. V.?

4. CASE OF MRS. WOODHULL AND MISS CLAFLIN.—These two sisters were, in 1872, publishing their "Weekly," a large sixteen-page paper, devoted to their peculiar views, and having a circulation of nearly ten thousand copies. They certainly had the same right to publish a paper that any other resident of the country possessed. They saw fit, in the fall of 1872, to publish intelligence in reference to what has since been known as the Beecher and Tilton scandal, but it was no more obscene than has been published in every daily paper in the city. Comstock caused their arrest in November, 1872. They were thrown into Ludlow Street Jail and their paper suppressed. Thus was a great wrong inflicted upon them as well as upon their numerous patrons in all parts of the country. They printed such a paper as their patrons approved of, and they had as much right to be served as any other portion of the community. Their paper was not only suppressed, but the printer and the stereotyper who did the work for the ladies were also arrested and subjected to great inconvenience.

Their bail was placed so high that they could not give it, and they were compelled to lie in prison many weeks prior to examination, the victims of the most bitter, intolerant spirit that ever ruled in this country. Their bail was divided up on different points, and, in the aggregate, is said to have amounted to over $80,000. It was the evident intention to keep them in prison without an examination, and thus suppress their paper.

In January, 1873, Mrs. Woodhull and Miss Claflin were again arrested and imprisoned, but, after several weeks, they were brought before Judge Blatchford of the U. S. Court, and he decided that they were illegally imprisoned, and that they had violated no law of the country. District Attorney Purdy proposed a *nolle prosequi* in the case, but their attorney objected, and the judge instructed the jury to find a verdict of acquittal, thus disposing of the case once for all, and preventing the prisoners being arrested again on the same charge.

This prosecution from first to last was a piece of cruel oppression towards those two women, and was wholly uncalled for. They had done nothing to merit such treatment from the Government. It damaged them to the extent of at least $20,000, and though they have applied to Congress to reimburse them for the great wrong done them, nothing has been yet effected. These women were unable to recover from the loss that had been unjustly imposed upon them.

5. GEORGE FRANCIS TRAIN was arrested in 1873 by Comstock on a charge of obscenity, and was thrown into the Tombs' damp, gloomy prison, where he lay in his close cell for six months. His offense consisted in publishing certain indecent passages from the Bible without a word of comment. It was evident that his accusers got ashamed of their conduct in arresting a highly intelligent man for publishing a limited number of extracts from the Bible in all their native purity. They wished to get him off their hands without a trial, but he refused to leave prison until duly tried and discharged. This they evaded. Finally, an order was issued from Albany to raze the unhealthy Tombs prison to the ground. Under this state of things Mr. Train left the prison, after which nothing was done toward tearing down the Tombs. To keep a citizen in prison so long, on so frivolous a charge, is a disgrace to the government and an outrage upon the rights of an American freeman.

6. CASE OF JOHN A. LANT.—In the spring of 1875 Mr. Lant moved his little paper, the "Toledo Sun," from Toledo, Ohio, to this city. It was a Freethought journal, and was far from immoral in its tone. It had not been here long, however, before it attracted the attention of Comstock, who resolved that it should be suppressed. He abused newsdealers on the sidewalk who presumed to sell the little paper, and he harshly threatened a friend of ours with imprisonment in the Tombs for selling the "Sun" containing Ingersoll's

"Oration on the Gods." After various devices, he sent an order to Mr. Lant for his paper, in the name of E. Semler, Green Farms, Conn., eulogizing the paper and urging Lant to press on in the good work he was doing. He ordered several back numbers, published before the paper was brought to New York. The most objectionable matter was a letter from Dr. E. P. Miller on physiological matters and a prayer by Train called "Beecher's Prayer." Some of the matter was not, perhaps, in the best possible taste, but there was nothing immoral in the papers.

Lant was thrown into Ludlow Street Jail and kept there two months, so as to effectually prevent the publication of his paper, and unexceptionable bail was refused. Finally, upon a writ of habeas corpus, Mr. Lant was removed from prison and admitted to bail, which was placed at $5,000. His final trial came off in December, his family suffering in the mean time for the very necessaries of life. His trial was short and severe. Comstock testified to writing the decoy letter in a fictitious name and receiving the "Sun" in return. The principal question raised at the trial was as to whether the matter objected to was obscene. The rulings of Judge Benedict were invariably against the accused. The charge to the jury was of the same hard, unfeeling character, and it was sufficient to induce a verdict of guilty, though not the slightest crime had been committed. The sentence was eighteen months at hard labor in the penitentiary at Albany, and $200 fine. Thus this man, in a feeble state of health, was torn from his wife and three little babes, who were wholly unprovided for, and at the commencement of winter. His prison life, with the labor that was imposed upon him, was very unfavorable to his health. He had, while there, some nineteen attacks of hemorrhage from the lungs and bronchial tubes. It is almost a marvel that he lived to serve out his time. When he returned to his family he was entirely without money and without business. This was an aggravated case, and shows to what length a spirit of persecution and intolerance may be carried in this so-called free America.

7. CASE OF SIMPSON.—This man kept a news and literary depot on Centre street, near Pearl street, for many years. It is not denied that he was an offender, and that in years past he sold works of an immoral character. It is not wished to defend him, or to apologize for him in this connection, but the case upon which he was tried and sentenced to ten years' imprisonment at hard labor, and a fine of five thousand dollars, seems one of extreme severity. Comstock got upon his track and was determined to place him in prison. He first caused his arrest for selling a card called the " picnic card," which was playful, but not immoral or vile. This was found insufficient. But not so a card referring to the marriage of Nellie Grant to Sartoris in the language of a naval engagement, without an absolutely obscene or immoral word in it. The issuing of this card which could not possibly do much harm to anybody, afforded sufficient grounds, under the laws of Congress, for Comstock to pursue the man, for the jury to find him guilty, and for the merciful Judge Benedict to sentence him to ten years' imprisonment at hard labor, and a fine of $5,000. In view of the trivial character of the offense, this seems to have been the severest sentence ever imposed in this country. Many a foul murderer, robber, thief, embezzler, defaulter, ravisher, calumniator, perjurer, or forger has gone scot-free, or with very insignificant punishment, while this man is compelled to spend ten years of his life in prison, at hard labor, with a fine of a sum larger than many earn in their whole lives hanging over him, and all for the selling of a card without an immodest word upon it. It seems almost incredible. Yet such is the truth. Under the Comstock laws almost anything is possible.

8. CASE OF HUNTER & Co.—This firm does an extensive publishing business at Hinsdale, N. H. Their paper, " The Star Spangled Banner," has a wide circulation. They also sell many books and miscellaneous goods. Anthony Comstock let his evil eye rest upon them, and he plotted their overthrow. He commenced operations by writing decoy letters from New Jersey (probably Squan Village), ordering

a simple French arrangement, sometimes called a "safe." This was the first one sold, and also the last, and this was sent by mail for Comstock's special benefit, though ordered under a false name. Anthony, thus armed and equipped, visited Hinsdale and arrested Mr. Hunter and four of his clerks, and had them carried off to be examined, though the clerks had nothing to do with the matter. He also seized and carried off a portion of their property, and ransacked the entire place to see if he could find anything obscene with which to feast his morbid appetite, but he found nothing of an improper character.

After Mr. Hunter had thus been spirited away, Comstock showed his extreme honesty and truthfulness by going to Mr. Hunter's dwelling and saying to Mrs. Hunter, "Mr. Hunter says you are to give me that package of fancy books." She knew nothing of anything of the kind, for the very good reason that there was nothing of the kind there. But, to increase his glory and renown with the members of the societies to which he belongs, he caused to be published in the Boston dailies, with flaming headings, accounts of the enormous seizures of obscene matter he had made in Hinsdale, claiming that it was the headquarters for villainy in the State. This was evidently done to prejudice public sentiment against Mr. Hunter, and to make it appear that he, Comstock, was doing a tremendous business in making seizures of matter of the most vile character.

Hunter & Co. have reason to be thankful that their case was not tried before the United States Circuit Court in this city. Had Judge Benedict been the judge before whom it was tried, the sending of that one simple, trivial apparatus, under his stern rulings, might easily have cost them two or more years' imprisonment and a fine of from three to five thousand dollars. As it was, though the case was not pressed against them, it cost them thousands of dollars, to the almost utter ruin of their business and an amount of trouble and intense anxiety on the part of themselves and families that never can be fully estimated. The most cruel and heartless part of the work of the informer in this case was his studied efforts to blacken their characters before the public by his false representations that tons of immoral and indecent matter were found upon their premises, when not the smallest part of it was true. Nothing immoral or obscene was found upon their premises, simply because it was not there. It is very easy to make false representations about others, and in this way to injure them to an incalculable extent; and a man who deliberately and maliciously does this, for the purpose of carrying out his own evil designs or to add to his own reputation and glory, ought to be shunned as the most dangerous fiend in the land.

9. DAVID MASSEY'S EXPERIENCE.—Mr. Massey was a merchant of St. Louis, and did a somewhat extensive and successful business until the war of the Rebellion. His business was largely in the South, and upon the breaking out of the war his trade was cut off, and thousands of dollars due him by his Southern customers could not be collected, and, like hundreds of others in similar cases, he was utterly ruined. He came to New York to find something to do. He obtained a clerkship with Rogers & Co., 737 Broadway, and there he became a victim to the wiles of Anthony Comstock, who sent a decoy letter to the house or to Mr. Massey, ordering some fancy pictures. Massey enclosed in an envelope a set of what were called "Black Crook" pictures, being representations of the ballet girls in costume as they appeared on the stage. Such pictures were very common in this city a few years ago, and stared passers-by in the face from scores of windows. A party who saw Massey put the pictures into the envelope will swear there was nothing obscene among them. But on the trial Comstock produced some very obscene pictures and swore he received them by mail from Massey. Mr. Massey contended in the strongest terms that Comstock committed perjury in his testimony against him, but it was sufficient to send him to prison for a year, with a fine of $500.

Without saying that Comstock committed perjury in this case, we can only say it was perfectly easy for him to do so.

Now it is submitted to the reader whether the liberty of American citizens is safe when a designing, dishonest, and unprincipled man, as Comstock has proved himself to be, and with a morbid fondness for sending people to prison, has the power, by his individual, uncorroborated testimony, to send hundreds of persons to prison, as he has publicly boasted of doing. It is extremely unsafe to place so much power as Comstock has wielded in the hands of a man like him.

The sister of Massey, heartbroken at the disgrace brought upon her brother and family, died, and was carried to an untimely grave. Mr. Massey left prison greatly impaired in health. He returned to St. Louis and was compelled to go to the hospital. When last heard from he was lying at the point of death. Another victim of the moral censor and spy, Anthony Comstock.

10. CASE OF DR. J. BOTT, AND OTHERS.—In the spring of 1872 Anthony Comstock made a trip to Washington and entered upon an enterprising, characteristic speculation, to which his talents and inclination so eminently adapt him. He rented post-office Box 260, provided himself with a lot of letter-heads belonging to the Treasury Department (which must have been dishonestly abstracted by himself or some other person), and wrote some eight or ten letters to as many physicians in this city. He assumed the character of a poor, unfortunate young girl who had been seduced and was in a condition to become a mother, and appealed in a most pitiful manner to those physicians to do something to relieve her. The following is a copy of the letter sent to one of the physicians, and upon comparison they were all found to be of the same tenor:

" WASHINGTON, D. C., March 18, 1873.

" DR. SELDEN—DEAR SIR: I am an employee of the Treasury and I have got myself into trouble. I was seduced about four months ago, and I am now about three months gone in the family way. The person who seduced me has run away and I do not know what will become of me if I do not get relief. I am a poor clerk and get only sixty dollars per month, and have to keep a widowed mother and a crippled sister, so that I send you all, in fact more than I can spare, hoping that you will send me something that will relieve me.

"Now, dear Doctor, send it right away, and send it by mail, for I do not want any one to have a breath of suspicion about the matter. For God's sake do not disappoint a poor ruined and forsaken girl whose only relief will be suicide if you fail me.

" Yours faithfully, MISS ANNA E. RAY.

" Please send package by mail to ' E. A. R.,' Box 260, Washington, D. C., and have it securely sealed."

Twenty dollars were placed in each letter and the same registered, so the parties receiving them were obliged to sign a receipt before obtaining the letter.

Letters of the same character were on the same day mailed to Dr. J. Bott, 84 Amity street; Dr. Alex. R. King, 10 Amity street; Dr. Dubois, 38 Great Jones street; Dr. Andrews, 45 Bleecker street; Dr. Marcus Jacoby, 161 Bleecker street. Dr. C. W. Selden, 67 Amity street. Such a cry of distress would move many a sympathetic heart to do something to afford relief, though no money was enclosed, but the two together were supposed sufficient to affect the stoutest heart.

Some of the physicians named suspected this was a " put up " case and sent nothing; others sent simple preparations, not calculated to produce any specific change in the person taking them, whether male or female. Others again, sent emmenagogue medicines adapted to the nature of the case.

Dr. Bott sent a simple powder of oxide of bismuth and powdered gentian, which is a simple stomachic and would not harm a woman in any condition. The prescription for the powder was filled at the drug-store on the corner of Sullivan and McDougal streets.

One of the physicians sent a box of common purgative pills, one sent pills and a decoction, and some, as observed, sent nothing. Comstock, having caught his game in the trap he had so skillfully set, came on to New York, feline-like, to play with them. He had all the physicians arrested who had sent him any medicines to get him out of the unpleasant condition which he represented himself to be in, and in due time they were brought to trial, convicted, and sent to prison. Dr. Jacoby was an exception; he had money. By paying $1,500 he escaped a trial and consequent imprisonment.

How much of that sum Anthony Comstock got, and where the balance found a lodging place, is not generally known.

When Dr. Bott was arrested he was cast into Ludlow Street Jail, where he lay six months before his trial came off, and when it did take place, it was a very summary affair. Comstock exhibited the registered letter receipt which Dr. Bott signed, a copy of the letter written, and the bismuth and gentian powder which the doctor sent him. Judge Benedict ruled that no other testimony was necessary, and refused to allow Dr. Bott, through his attorney, James D. McClelland, Esq., to introduce testimony to show the simple nature of the powder sent, which he wished to do by the druggist who prepared it. He ruled that the doctor's sending any powder in response to Comstock's fraudulent decoy letter was *prima facie* evidence of his guilt, and peremptorily charged the jury to find a verdict of guilty, which they did without leaving their seats.

The sentence of Dr. Bott was eighteen months in Crow Hill penitentiary, Brooklyn, which, with the six months in Ludlow Street Jail, made two years, for the heinous crime of sending through the mail a simple stomachic powder, and which he never would have sent had not Comstock decoyed him to do so.

One who has not tasted the bitterness of prison life cannot fully appreciate its ills. Dr. Bott lost an arm in the late war. Being naturally a man of fine sensibilities, he was broken down and crushed by the weight of the great misfortune that befell him, and so were his family. They were disgraced and outraged. The doctor's health gave way under the hardship and deprivation of prison life. He was sick while in prison, and came out a mere wreck of his former self. He subsequently passed a considerable portion of his time in hospitals ; his health was ruined and his spirit completely broken down. In December, 1877, the writer visited his bedside during the closing hours of his life. He died the following night. As the writer watched him drawing his few remaining breaths, he instinctively exclaimed, " This is but another result of the

American Inquisition. This is the finale of another unfortunate victim of Anthony Comstock's cruelty and greed."
This case of Dr. Bott's is thought to be at least the twentieth
in which Comstock, by his relentless prosecutions and persecutions, has sent the victim to an untimely grave as surely as
though he had shot him or stabbed him to the heart.

11. CASE OF MR. KENDALL.—This man was a dealer in
rubber goods. Comstock, by a decoy letter, induced Kendall
to send him by mail a rubber female syringe, a useful and
valuable instrument. For this enormous crime he was
arrested and disgraced, thrown into prison, kept there for six
months, and his business entirely ruined.

12. CASE OF MR. WEIL.—This gentleman was a photographer, pursuing the even tenor of his way on Broadway, New
York, not far from Twelfth street. He was a quiet, well-dis-
posed citizen, but Comstock fain would ruin him. Comstock,
in person, or by his deputy, visited his gallery in search of
improper photographs. Weil informed him that he made
nothing of the kind. "But will you make them if I bring
you the negatives?" "No, sir; I wish to do nothing of the
kind." But finally Comstock discovered in the gallery an
artistic photograph which Weil had taken of his own little
boy in undress. This, in Comstock's eyes, was a heinous
offense against the peace and morality of the country. The
photographer's negatives were seized, his property carried off,
and he was subjected to much trouble and considerable
expense.

In a similar way many photograph galleries were raided,
and negatives and apparatus to the value of thousands of
dollars forcibly carried away. The censor and protector of
public morals deemed photographs of classic statuary and
paintings grossly obscene, and this was a sufficient incentive
for him to seize and remove negatives, instruments, etc. In
this way many photographers were seriously wronged.

It is reported that victims have been arrested, tried, and
imprisoned for sending through the mails photographs and
prints of statuary like Power's Greek Slave, the original of

which hundreds of thousands have viewed with the purest and grandest emotions of pleasure.

13. CASE OF DR. WILLIAM MORRISON. — One of Comstock's feats was bringing this worthy gentleman into serious trouble. He is an Englishman, but was twenty years in this city, and is most respectably connected, both in England and in this country. He kept a drug-store at 515 Pearl street, and connected with that store for many years had been a trade in what was called "French Remedies and Goods." Comstock had his evil eye, or possibly his pious eye, on the doctor, and secretly worked his downfall. He wrote letters simulating a young lady in the upper part of the city, asking for certain articles forbidden by the laws to be sent through the mails, to which the doctor promptly replied that the trade was in violation of law and he would have nothing to do with it.

In October, 1877, Comstock renewed his epistolary correspondence with Dr. Morrison. This time he simulated a young lady by the name of Ella Bender, of Squan Village, N. J. She wrote a very confidential letter to the doctor and asked for some information or some remedy that would prevent her being unfortunately caught should she be exposed. The doctor simply enclosed in an envelope an old leaf of an advertisement referring to Hooper's Female Pills, which have been a standard medicine for a hundred years, and are not capable of doing much good or harm.

"Miss Ella" again wrote more affectionately and confidentially to the doctor, speaking to him in very endearing language, chiding him for his want of gallantry in not writing her and signing his name to the letter. She in plain language informed the doctor that she was under the necessity of making a living in the best way she could, and that sometimes she had to do certain things a little against her will, and she wished him to send her some of those "French appliances" that would keep her safe and sound. He replied that it was against the law to send anything of the kind by mail, and he should not do so. Again she wrote the doctor, growing still more affectionate and urgent in her appeals, and informing him that her sister would probably buy some of the same kind of goods if he would send her one of his circulars. She wrote four letters in all, at which time the doctor was so far seduced by her artfulness as to send her a pessary and a " safe."

This was enough to do the business. The crafty hypocrite and falsifier had met with the success which his heart coveted. He at once took steps to arrest the doctor with the view of immuring him within the walls of a prison. He visited the doctor's place of business, accompanied by a United States deputy-marshal who had borne him company upon many a similar errand of cruelty, heartlessness, injustice, and terror. It was soon made apparent that Miss Ella Bender, the Squan Village girl who wanted to buy some "French fixings" that she might engage in certain liaisons without danger to herself, and Mr. Anthony Comstock, the eminent Christian, the noted agent, inquisitor, and detective for the United States Government, the agent and secretary of the Society for the Suppression of Vice, and the pet champion of the Y. M. C. A., were one and the same person. Miss Ella, instead of being a dashing, fascinating brunette of the female persuasion, turned out to be a coarse, burly, hard-cheeked, sandy-haired, merciless masculine, with a frightful scar on the left side of his face inflicted while he was making an illegal arrest by the one-armed Conroy.

While on that friendly call at the doctor's, Comstock, in rummaging a private drawer in a writing-table, played the sharp game of abstracting the letters which the sweet "Ella" had written to her "Dear Doctor," and carried them away with him.

The information respecting this case was obtained from Dr. Morrison, direct. He was duly indicted and tried, before Judge Benedict and a verdict of guilty, upon Comstock's evidence, was rendered against him. At the instance of the doctor's lawyer, sentence was deferred, and the doctor, fearing it might be too severe, determined to forfeit his bail and leave for Europe, so Comstock did not have the pleasure of sending this man to prison. Dr. Morrison stated emphatically that Comstock in giving his evidence in the case perverted the truth. Whether or not this was so the writer has no means of knowing; but putting on the best possible construction of the case in Comstock's favor, it was one of criminal duplicity, falsehood, and intrigue; Comstock used decoy letters, false signatures, and so forth, and induced the old doctor to commit an offense that he otherwise would not have thought of committing.

14. CASE OF CHARLES CONROY.—Conroy is a one-handed man, having been born without a right hand. He made a living by selling books and pamphlets, mostly of Dick & Fitzgerald's publications, being song books, dream books, books of games, letter writers, books of etiquette, and so forth. He did business in this city, and also in Newark, N. J. It was in the latter city that Comstock commenced his attack upon him. Conroy did an advertising business, and had letters sent to him in different names. Comstock, deeming this a great offense, applied to the U. S. Commissioner in Newark for a warrant for the arrest of Conroy. The Commissioner, however, not deeming the matter complained of as being sufficient to justify the issuing of a warrant, refused to do so, whereupon Comstock decided to arrest Conroy without a warrant. He accordingly arrested him without the slightest color of authority, taking him forcibly and hustling him into a covered carriage, and drove off without ceremony, and took him before the commissioner, who held him for examination. While Conroy was being conveyed to prison he told Comstock that he had arrested him without the slightest authority and with no warrant. Comstock's reply was, "If I do not succeed in convicting you on this arrest, I will follow you up until I get you into prison." As they neared the prison and Conroy saw its grim walls looming up before him, he remembered his wife and child at home, and how they would be left to suffer while he was immured within prison walls, and he realized how unjust and cruel the arrest was. He took his little pocket-knife, the only weapon he had, and with his left

hand gave Comstock one blow upon his left cheek, cutting a bad gash nearly two inches in length. Comstock recovering himself, hastily pulled his pistol from his pocket and placed it at Conroy's head, and at that instant the carriage door was opened and the jailer appeared with another pistol, which he also presented unpleasantly near Conroy's head. Thus, with a pistol on each side of his head, the overpowered man with a single hand, deemed submission the wiser part and, he was placed in a cell. He was tried upon the charge of committing an atrocious assault upon an officer. Comstock, of course, appeared against him and with his testimony obtained a verdict of two years' imprisonment in the State prison at Trenton. On the day the prisoner was sentenced, some twenty of Comstock's bosom friends, members of the Young Men's Christian Association, went from New York to Newark to witness the interesting proceedings. And when the prisoner had been conducted to the State prison at Trenton, Comstock took the trouble to make a journey there to impress upon the keeper or warden that Conroy was a very dangerous man and ought to be kept in the closest confinement, in pursuance of which advice Conroy was confined in a very close uncomfortable cell during the hottest weather. When his term had expired, and before he had left the steps of the prison, Comstock was on hand, and had him again arrested on the original charge of receiving letters in a fictitious name, had him tried, convicted, and sentenced to another year in prison. This statement was obtained from Conroy himself.

The cut which he inflicted on Comstock's face was somewhat serious, bleeding badly on his way home and weakening him considerably. But his Christian friends being very sympathetic with him, in consideration of the great peril he had been placed in, and the danger he had incurred in the cause of morality and justice, made him up a purse of several thousand dollars for his great suffering and loss of blood. This entire case was one of aggravated injustice and wrong

Comstock's attention has not been wholly given to suppressing dealers in contraband literature and tabooed articles.

He has been as much opposed to physicians and medical authors who presumed to write and publish medical works heterodox in character as to heterodoxy in religion.   He has worked as much in the interests of the "regular" school of physicians as of the regular school of theologians. Let it once be known that a physician was publishing a popular medical work, which presumed to step aside from the beaten track of regular practice and Comstock considered him as his legitimate "game." He pursued such with the same relentless rapacity as other classes of offenders.   A few such cases will be given as samples of many others for which there hardly is room.

15. CASE OF DR. E. B. FOOTE.—This was an instance where the greatest injustice and cruelty were inflicted upon one of the purest, best, and most amiable of men, whose life has been spent in instructing and improving his fellow-beings by giving them such information as is well calculated to aid them to be more healthy, more happy, and better and more useful men and women.   His medical works possess the highest value, and have been introduced into hundreds of thousands of families, which to-day stand ready to bear testimony to the great benefit they have derived from the physiological, hygienic, and moral lessons which he has so ably imparted.

His character is elevated, and his desire is to elevate and benefit his fellow-beings.   In his medical experience, running over a third of a century, no man can truthfully charge him with an action prompted by an improper motive, or with an attempt to procure an abortion or anything of the kind.   His course has been singularly free from everything of the kind, and it is only alluded to because of the efforts on the part of a cruel persecutor and prosecutor to cast this vile stigma upon him.   The cries of "mad dog" and "abortionist" are easily raised by those who would willingly inflict wrong upon the deserving; but how unjust to do so when there is not the slightest grounds for such conduct!

Dr. Foote was an unfortunate victim of a designing,

unscrupulous, relentless persecutor. Because he has been considered not fully *orthodox* in his medical status, because he has presumed to give highly valuable instruction as to how some of the greatest evils of society may be morally and legitimately obviated, the ire of his prosecutor was aroused against him. He was seized as a criminal and as a disseminator of unclean literature; he was falsely charged; he was obliged to give bail to avoid being thrust into prison; the most intense anxiety and unhappiness were forced upon him, upon his estimable wife, his aged mother, who resides with him, and upon his children and his friends; he was forced to stand trial in a court where the utmost severity is the rule, and where the strict construction of an unjust law was made to bear heavily upon him; thousands upon thousands of dollars were stripped from him; his business injured to the extent of fully $25,000, and an amount of that intense anxiety and apprehension which cannot be estimated by dollars and cents, and which no person can realize who has not been made to experience it. All this has been brought upon a man who had not committed a fault—who had not done the first thing towards violating the laws of honor, virtue, or morality.

For some twenty years Dr. Foote has employed the few moments he could snatch from professional labors in writing such physiological works as he sincerely believed were needed by the people—in 1857–8, "Medical Common Sense;" in 1869–70, "Plain Home Talk," embracing the main features of the first book; in 1874–5, "Science in Story," which has received commendation, not only from the secular but from the religious press. Thus far the work has received no adverse criticism. In these works, and in pamphlets issued from time to time, the doctor has labored to show the necessity of improving humanity by having no children born the creatures of accident; in other words, has treated indirectly and directly, in nearly all the works he has written, on the importance of scientific propagation, no less in the human family than on the stock-farm. That is to say, this has been one feature of his writings. The consideration of this important subject naturally led to the devising and prescribing of effective means for making what John Stuart Mill called " conjugal prudence " possible in all cases wherein disease was to be entailed on offspring, or indeed in all instances wherein the reproductive function might better be rendered inoperative. This information was imparted in a pamphlet entitled " Words in Pearl for the Married," which was prepared for the purpose of answering a score of questions which are asked daily of a physician in extensive practice. To make it as unobjectionable as possible, it was set up in pearl type, so as to make it only thirty-two pages of about the size of a letter envelope, in which it was invariably sent *sealed, under letter postage.* Its object in great part was to save letter-writing when questions were asked, which its pages directly answered. The pamphlet took strong grounds against producing miscarriage or abortion. When the postal obscene-literature law was passed, some of its pages, referring to the prevention of conception, in conflict with the new statute, were promptly expurgated. Shortly after the Congressional law was enacted, a similar one was passed in our own State, forbidding the devising or supplying of any means whatever for the prevention of conception. The doctor was assured by his legal adviser that this clause would never be enforced against physicians; but not being a member of the conservative school of medicine, and his advice often being sought upon a subject so intimately connected with his pet hobby of scientific propagation, he thought best to put himself upon a legal footing both in respect to the Congressional and State laws. In doing this he followed legal advice.

Nevertheless, in January, 1876, he was suddenly and unexpectedly called upon to give bonds in the sum of $5,000 for his appearance before the United States Court, an indictment having been found against him, at the instigation of Mr. Comstock, for sending an alleged obscene pamphlet and notices of preventive articles through the United States mail. It appears that these were sent, in answer to a decoy letter, to a Mrs. Semler in Chicago, who, in her application, expressed great admiration for the doctor's "Plain Home Talk." Orders of this character, however, seldom came to the personal notice of the doctor. They belonged to the order department, where the clerk in charge had, without consultation with or permission from his employer, sufficiently changed his arrangements to place him in a questionable position before this iron-clad law. First, it was confidently believed a *nolle prosequi* would be entered by the prosecuting attorney; next that the indictment would be quashed; and finally, when the case came unexpectedly to trial, on the twenty-first of June, acquittal was fully expected up to the moment when the jury retired for their decision on the twenty-sixth; even the prosecuting attorney, it is said, looked for nothing better for his side than a disagreement of the jury. It was, therefore, a matter of great surprise when the jury, after an absence of only twenty minutes, returned with a verdict of guilty! The rulings of the judge were peculiar. The defense, while believing that the pamphlet was not obscene, considered it a strong point that the publication was only sent through the mails sealed and under letter postage. Judge Benedict in his charge turned this point against the defense by saying substantially that those who would not buy such a work over a counter could obtain it in a sly way through the mails. Although the order clerk distinctly testified that he had sent the notice through the mails on his own responsibility, and with no permission from his employer, the judge charged that the principal should be held responsible the same as a bank officer would be for a notice of protest issued by a subordinate! Judge Benedict further said that medical works need not be sent by mail; that they could be sent by express; seeming to ignore the fact that the peculiar statute not only prohibited certain publications from going through the mails, but any notices in print or writing stating where such publications could be obtained.

After the rendition of the verdict, bail was doubled to $10,-000, for which the doctor must find bondsmen or go to prison. Counsel were sure that Judge Benedict under the circumstances would not impose a fine of perhaps more that $100. The prisoner was a physician; the pamphlet was nothing more than advice which is orally given by every well-known practitioner to his inquiring patients. These circumstances, together with the unauthorized character of the notices, would be considered.

The judge was urged by personal appeal and written to by anxious friends and patients of the doctor to deal leniently with him. Among the letters passed through the hands of his attorneys to Judge Benedict was one from an ex-governor, who said he knew the prisoner to be " an excellent citizen, a man of studious habits and pure life ;" one from a physician of prominence in the homœopathic school, a professor in one of its universities, and a high officer in one of its societies, who said he was satisfied of Dr. Foote's " genial humanitarianism, keen intellect, and honest purpose ;" one from an independent physician, graduate of a first-class allopathic university, and ex-professor of several medical universities, who remarked that " physicians generally agree that the pamphlet contains nothing but candid and rational answers to questions usually asked," and so forth ; one from a noted clergyman, who expressed his hearty approval of the Doctor's publications, including his pamphlet, and who said he had placed two sets of " Science in Story " in his Sunday-school library : one from a sculptor whose work in artistic bronze beautifies one of the rambles in Central Park ; one from an old and honored publisher, who originally brought out Harriet Beecher Stowe's " Uncle Tom's Cabin ;" one from a professor high in the eclectic medical profession, together with many others, all testifying to the fact that the doctor was entitled to mercy. On the eleventh day of July, while thousands of people were crowding the Centennial Exposition in commemoration of the birth of this great *free* republic, Dr. Foote was fined $3,500 for publishing a little work which a large number of intelligent and reputable physicians and thousands of good people throughout the United States believed to contain only such information as at least every adult had a right to know !

(Sentence was not passed for sending the notices.) It was fully believed by the doctor and his friends that this victim of a clumsy statute barely escaped the State prison! The fine and costs of defense exceeded $5,000. The developments during the trial led many to the conviction that the law and its agents were being employed by conservative members of the profession to destroy a Liberal medical writer and practitioner. Circumstances have come to the knowledge of the doctor since the summer of 1876 which have led him reluctantly to believe that these suspicions, in which he was too charitable at the time to share, were well founded. At all events, it was a case of great injustice and illiberal tyranny on the part of a bigoted Christian society and their overzealous agent.

16. CASE OF DR. E. C. ABBEY.—Dr. Abbey is a resident of the city of Buffalo, and is a gentleman of the highest intelligence and moral worth. He graduated in 1861, thus having been a legal medical practitioner for more than a sixth of a century. He is a prominent member of the Masonic fraternity, and enjoys a first-class reputation among the wide number who know him, and is thoroughly indorsed by the best men of all classes in whose midst he has dwelt for many years.

He has written and published a work on the sexual system and its derangements. Sexual diseases have been made a specialty by him; which study was induced by what he witnessed in this connection while pursuing his collegiate studies. When about to issue his work, he placed the manuscript in the hands of the district attorney, who pronounced it legal and not in conflict with any law. After its publication he submitted it to the best medical counsel in the State of New York, as well as the best legal talent, including the Hon. Daniel F. Day and others, who pronounced the work all right from a legal point of view and one whose circulation would, as calculated, do a great amount of good. He had not the slightest motive to issue an improper or an immoral book, and he took every precaution to obtain legal and able counsel upon the subject. A copy was taken to U. S. Commissioner Fillmore, son of ex-President Fillmore, who declined to entertain the case at all. Before another commissioner the result was different. Anthony Comstock's attention was called to Dr. Abbey's work, and, as it imparts to the masses information upon the important subjects of human physiology and the laws of health, he decided it was an improper work to receive mail facilities. His detective commenced operations. Decoy letters were employed. Dr. Abbey sent a copy of this work to Comstock, giving all the facts about its publication, the names of men of standing who had endorsed the doctor's character, and asked the conservator of the public morals of America to state his objections to it. He assured Comstock also that an arrest and trial were unnecessary ; that he was ready to make any modification deemed necessary.

It was perhaps an error on the part of Dr. Abbey to take this course. He was arrested and his books seized as obscene. This was unquestionably a high-handed outrage. They should not have been seized as obscene until pronounced to be of that character by proper legal authorities. Comstock, however, considered himself competent to decide what is obscene, and any popular work designed to circulate among the masses, and which gave any information upon the subject of human physiology, he pronounced obscene. He has said, in his very positive and offensive manner, "No works on physiology shall be allowed to go through the mails." The rights and liberties of American citizens have indeed sunk to a low point if a man of the very moderate literary and scientific acquirements of Anthony Comstock shall become censor of the public press and the United States mail, and shall have the power to say what books the people may read, and what they may not read, what they may send and receive through the mail, and what not! Was it for this kind of liberty that our fathers fought and bled in the days of the Revolution ? Was it for this kind of universal freedom that the great struggle was made to sustain our Government in the late rebellion ?

The wrong thus perpetrated against Dr. Abbey by seizing his property and holding it without legal authority was continued nearly three years, his books, as understood, being thus wrongfully and unjustly detained. When taken before Judge Wallace of the U. S. District Court, Dr. Abbey very promptly admitted that he had deposited his medical work in the mail and that he was proud of having done so, regarding the same distinctly as his right and duty. He raised objections to the indictment as not being specific, and claimed firmly but respectfully that his work was not in any sense an obscene book. The jury that tried him were fresh from their barns and firesides, and were unfortunately of a class incompetent to judge of the merits of a medical work. They had not, in fact, read enough of works of that kind to constitute them capable judges of their true merits. The District Attorney read a few isolated passages which, to the unlettered minds of such a jury as are often seen sitting to try matters they do not understand, sounded plain and reprehensible, and late on Saturday evening, when they were tired and anxious to return home, they readily decided the case adversely, and in five minutes found that valuable medical work an obscene book.

This was another instance of high-handed outrage upon a worthy citizen who presumed to impart information to his fellow-beings that they ought to have and which he was fully able to give. But he was not within the medical " ring," and hence his troubles.

Other physicians in St. Louis, Indianapolis, and other cities, have been annoyed in a similar way by Comstock, suffering heavy damages at his hands, but their cases will be passed over.

To enable this representative of the Young Men's Christian Association to perform his dirty work, he has found it necessary to have an accomplice and assistant. The person who has filled this position is Joseph A. Britton, alias Cohen, alias Andrews, alias Levy, etc. He is said to be a renegade Jew, who now claims to be a member of a Christian church. That he is base enough to be a fitting tool and companion to

Anthony Comstock there cannot be the slightest doubt. The two have worked together to ensnare and beguile unwary persons to commit offenses for which they could be arraigned before the American Inquisition, the United States Courts. Often has Britton endeavored to buy obscene books and pictures, and often has he filled his pockets with the vile trash and tried to sell them to simple-minded dealers. If the talent and industry these two men have given to the execrable business they have engaged in could have been bestowed in a more worthy direction, it would have been far better for them and all concerned. They are eminently worthy of each other. A few cases which the spies and informers have jointly worked up, will be given:

17. CASE OF JOHN MANNING.—Manning is a young man, and, in 1875, started a little news and literary stand on the corner of New Chambers and Pearl streets. He had been open but a short time when he received visits from Comstock's assistant, Britton. He bought papers, etc., of Manning, and called in from week to week, until he became well acquainted, and was regarded by Manning as a friend. Britton on one occasion asked for fancy photographs. Manning told him he had none, and that he had never dealt in anything of the kind. "But," said Britton, "cannot you get some for me? If you have an opportunity to pick up any, save them for me, and I will pay you a good price." This request was repeated several times, and Manning told him if he saw anything of the kind he would get them. Some time after this he had an opportunity to buy some photographs of nude figures, statuary, etc., and thinking they might suit his friend Britton, he purchased them for him. He did not deem it best to keep them in his store, but put them in his trunk at his boarding-house. Britton called soon after and was told he had some photographs for him. "Keep them," said Britton; "I will call again and take them." When he next called, Comstock accompanied him, and remained outside the place while his accomplice went in to work the ruin of young Manning. The latter told the villain Britton

that the pictures were not in his store, and that he would have to lock up his place and go over to his lodging-house, which he did, Britton accompanying him. As soon as he got outside, Britton signaled to Comstock that he had the pictures, and Comstock immediately arrested the unsuspecting young man, without a warrant or the slightest authority, and dragged him off to prison. The trial and conviction followed in due time. Comstock appeared against the accused, and swore that certain pictures were taken off the person of Manning which Manning affirms he never saw till Comstock produced them in court and swore them on to him. Manning will take his oath that this is the truth. He was sentenced to one year's imprisonment; and a stigma and disgrace was thus designedly and shamefully placed upon the young man that will injure him for life. It is a most disgraceful charge to be imprisoned for selling obscene pictures. One thing, however, is certain, this young man would not have thought of engaging in that kind of traffic had he not been repeatedly urged to do so by the accomplice of this agent for the Y. M. C. A. and the Society for the Suppression of Vice.

18. CASE OF A. PROSCH.—Mr. Prosch is a worthy gentleman, sixty-four years of age. His life has been beyond reproach and singularly free from all objectionable practices. He has never drank liquor or used tobacco, he has never attended theatres, or played a game of cards, and has been unusually careful to avoid bad company and to shun even the appearance of evil. He has lived a quiet, unobtrusive life, and no one can justly speak ill of him. He is an artistic mechanic and manufacturer of stereopticons or magic-lanterns. He was formerly in business in Chatam Square, and is now on the corner of Division and Catherine streets, New York. His shop is filled with lathes and other implements and machinery with which, with one or two assistants, he manufactured the instruments that so highly interest and instruct thousands of people.

In the spring of 1877 he was induced by Mr. Daniel Walford, an active member of two temperance organizations, to attend their social society meeting and edify them with the exhibition of one of his stereopticons. It was not his custom to exhibit his instruments in this way; in fact, this was the first instance of the kind. He was simply a manufacturer; but in this instance, to amuse a social party of temperance people, he consented to spend an evening with them and minister to their pleasure; and this he did without fee or compensation. The pictures used were chaste and moral, a portion of which were of statuary and ancient paintings, embracing, of course, some nude figures; none were from life. Many gentlemen and their wives were present, and everybody was pleased, and none were in the least shocked by the exhibition. There was, however, one person present whose impure mind caught at the idea that as nude figures from statuary, and so forth, had been represented, it would be a good chance for Comstock to work up a case. He reported the affair to Britton, the accomplice and confidential assistant of Comstock, who at an early moment communicated the intelligence to his master, and he was instructed to give his attention to the case and to work it up. Britton visited Mr. Prosch and said, with words of lying hypocrisy in his mouth, "I understand, Mr. Prosch, that a few evenings ago you gave before a temperance society a very interesting exhibition of pictures and engravings with one of your instruments. Now, I called to see you about giving a similar exhibition before a political club to which I belong. We are going to have a special meeting soon, and I wish to engage you to be with us with your stereopticon and pictures." To which Mr. Prosch replied, "It is not my business to exhibit my instruments; I manufacture them. I went the other evening to please and amuse some friends, and it is the only instance where I have done so." "Well," said Britton, "I hope you will not refuse also to come for us. We will pay you liberally for your time and trouble, and you will afford us much amusement."

Mr. Prosch thus importuned, and thinking perhaps he could make a few dollars for the evening's labor, consented to go, whereupon Britton plied the unsuspecting man on this tack : " Now, you see our club is composed mostly of young men, and we are fond of something rich and a little gay. Those pictures you have exhibited are well enough, but can't you get something for us a little 'stronger' or more fancy?" " No," said Mr. Prosch, " I don't know that I can. Those are all the pictures I have." " But, my friend," said the detective, " we are willing to pay you liberally if you will get something to please us. Can you not make an effort to find something of the style we want?" " Well, yes ; maybe so," answered the old man, weakening, perhaps, at the thought of making an extra dollar or two. " I will try and see what I can do for you." The Christian detective said he would call again.

In a short time the detective called again, in fact, he called several times on this business, and was very importunate and looked over the addition the manufacturer had made to his stock, with which he pronounced himself well pleased. He then renewed the engagement for their exhibition before his club, to take place on a certain night.

Then the vigilant detective reported to his chief, the veritable Comstock, how successfully he had roped in the old man, and how he had induced him to procure pictures that might be called obscene. Comstock soon put in an appearance at the old man's shop and asked to see the pictures, saying he was one of the club before which he was to exhibit. When this agent of the Christian Association had piously inspected the pictures which the old man had, which his hypocritical tool had persuaded the good man to procure, and which he never would have purchased save for such persuasion, he, like a fiend, turned upon the innocent, harmless old man, and said : " Now I have you. You are my prisoner. Accompany me at once."

Mr. Prosch was working at his lathe, in his shirt-sleeves and slippers, with his apron on. Said he, " If I must go with you, let me put on my coat and boots, and not be compelled to go through the streets in this way." " No," replied Comstock, imperiously ; " come along at once, or I will prefer the additional charge against you of resisting an officer of the

Government." And thus that inoffensive old man of sixty-four years was, on a cold day in April, compelled by Comstock to march along the streets of this city without his coat; and, when one of his employees followed with it, Comstock would not allow the old man to stop and put it on; and not until he reached the police station and was placed in the charge of a policeman was a kind word spoken to him or was he allowed to put on his coat to keep out the cold.

The arrest was made late in the afternoon, and when he had been examined before the proper authorities it was too late to procure bail, and Mr. Prosch was compelled to pass the night in the Oak street station house. There was nothing in his cell to sleep upon save a hard plank, and in his perturbed state of mind at the sudden change in his fortunes, he trod his narrow cell all night, without a moment's sleep coming to his eyelids. This was purposely planned by the agent of the Young Men's Christian Association; and, as it turned out, the unhappy old man had to pass the second night in that dismal cell before acceptable bail could be procured. In the meantime Mr. Prosch's invalid wife was rendered extremely wretched by the absence of her husband, and that he was detained upon such a disgraceful charge. She could not bear to have her nearest friends know what the charge was, and the grief she felt nearly crushed her into the grave. She has, with tears, described to the writer the extreme grief the event caused her, and she did not believe she could live to pass through another such trial.

The case duly went before the grand jury, and a bill was found against Mr. Prosch. But the affair is still unsettled, after having cost the old man a great amount of anxiety, damaging his reputation, nearly breaking up his business, and costing him fully a thousand dollars in money he was illy able to spare. It is still held in terror over his head, and nearly destroys his happiness and that of his sick wife, who, if her husband is convicted upon so disgraceful a charge, will be hurried to her grave. When Mr. Walford, his wife, and other prominent members of the temperance organization, went to Mr. Comstock with the endeavor to soften his severity towards the poor, unfortunate man, and said that they persuaded him to exhibit his pictures before their society, that he had charged nothing, and that there was not the slightest impropriety in the exhibition, and that both gentlemen and ladies were highly pleased with it, they found this protector of American decency and morality implacable and unyielding, and he seemed determined to pursue the harmless old man to the very death for committing what he (Comstock) was pleased to consider a crime, and which the old man would never have thought of committing had he not been persuaded into it by Comstock's own directions and by one of his own lackeys.

Friends of Mr. Prosch also called upon Mr. Samuel Colgate, president of the Society for the Suppression of Vice, and laid before him the outrageous manner in which Comstock had managed this case. Mr. Colgate was evidently appalled at the deception and unfeeling cruelty that had been practiced upon the old man, and through his efforts the case was pigeon-holed and has never been called up.

This affair is a disgrace to American liberty and Christian morality; and few of the cases of persecution in the past centuries, considering the time and place, were more criminal, cruel, and relentless.

19. CASE OF CHARLES F. BLANDIN.—This gentleman is a lawyer, and, in 1877, moved from Boston to New York, with the intention of following his profession in the metropolis; but finding business dull, he temporarily engaged at canvassing for a stationary and printing house. While thus employed he unfortunately called at the office of Anthony Comstock. Here he found the accomplice, Britton, who was exceedingly affable and talkative, and, ere the interview was closed, he made known his desire to procure some fancy pictures, and handed Blandin a card, which read thus, "Joseph B. Andrews, buyer of rare, rich, and racy books and photographs, &c., Philadelphia," representing himself to be Andrews, and a dealer in that kind of goods. Blandin

replied that he dealt in nothing of the kind and knew nothing about such goods. Britton repeatedly urged him to try and find something of the kind, and extracted a promise from him that if he (Blandin) succeeded in finding anything of the kind he would let Britton know.

Some two months after this Blandin made a visit to Boston and upon meeting an old friend was casually shown some six or eight fancy photographs. They were the first he had ever seen. The promise he had made to Britton come to his mind and he begged his friend to lend him one of the pictures to show to Britton on his return to New York. When he did return he called at 150 Nassau street, but finding Britton out he left a note, saying he had called to fulfill his promise. Soon after this Britton called at Blandin's office and left a note requesting Blandin to call again, at an hour named, at 150 Nassau street. Unfortunately, Blandin called. Comstock and Britton were both in. They were much pleased with the picture, and wanted a thousand. Blandin informed them he had but the one, which he had borrowed to show Andrews, as he had promised, and that he must return that to its owner, and that was all he would have, saying it was not for sale, and that he knew not where they could be obtained. He replaced the picture in his pocket and started to leave, but was called back and further plied with questions. Britton took possession of the picture, and, upon Blandin's reaching out his hand to regain possession of it, Britton, instead of returning the picture, put thirty cents in Blandin's hand, saying "I want to keep this picture. You can obtain all of them you want; here are thirty cents to pay you for the trouble of bringing this in." Blandin refused to accept the money, and demanded his picture, offering the money back. At this juncture Comstock stepped from his private room or office and interrupted the dispute. He brandished a club and exhibited his badge of office, and, placing his hand in a ruffianly manner upon Blandin's shoulder, said: "You are my prisoner; my name is Comstock. Now tell me where you obtained that picture." Although Blandin might have thereby obtained his liberty he refused to divulge his friend's name. The unsuspecting victim was immediately marched to the tombs without being permitted to visit his office and leave word of his arrest. He was a stranger in the city and could not give bail. He lay in prison thirteen weeks awaiting trial, when, upon the unsupported testimony of Comstock and Britton, he was convicted. The jury, deeming him guiltless of intentional wrong, recommended him to the mercy of the court. His sentence was made the lowest prescribed by the law, to wit, three months' imprisonment and $100 fine. He was sent to the penitentiary, where his companions were the vilest characters known. His situation was deplorable. His attorney, B. F. Russell, who had known him ten years and that he was a person of good moral character, and had defended him without fee, visited Albany, and laid the case before the governor, who, feeling that a wrong had been done an inno-cent person, and that this was more a case of cruel persecution than of legal prosecution, sent his son down from Albany to investigate the case. The judge, the foreman of the grand jury, and the jury signed the petition for pardon, but Comstock did all in his power to prevent it, and brought out the volumi-nous credentials from his Society for the Suppression of Vice. But all his efforts were in vain. The governor upon learning all the facts in the case, and becoming convinced of the wrong that had been perpetrated, had the good sense and mercy to grant a full and unconditional pardon. Too much cannot be said in praise of the governor who took so noble a stand in defense of an injured individual, an oppressed citizen who was made to seemingly have committed a crime by a designing, unscrupulous, and relentless prosecutor. Blandin had not intended and did not intend to violate any law of virtue, honor, or morality.

Thus was Comstock rebuked. And, notwithstanding the stigma which has been thrown for life upon Blandin by being arrested for selling an obscene picture, we deem him a far bet-ter man than Comstock, and far less deserving of imprison-ment.

The New York "World" for March 11, 1878, besides giving the details of Blandin's trial and conviction as above had these comments on the case.

"It is not a pretty story which appears in our columns to-day of an arrest just made by Mr. Comstock, with the help of an assistant who clearly seems to have seduced the offender into committing the offense for which he was arrested. There can be no baser or more mischievous crime in its way against society than this, and if the respectable members of the association by which Mr. Comstock is understood to be employed desire to preserve their own good name and the reputation of the work in which they are engaged, they will lose no time in clearing themselves of the very serious scandal brought upon both by such proceedings as those which were Saturday testified to before Judge Sutherland.

20. CASE OF LOUIS WENGENRATH.—This man for several years kept a confectionery in the eastern part of Brooklyn, and was regarded as an honorable man, and entitled to the respect of all who knew him. His connections were good, and he moved in good society. Joseph A. Britton, the accomplice and tool of Anthony Comstock, for a long time had been in the habit of calling upon the confectioner, and making slight purchases of him. In February, 1878, this unprincipled man said to the confectioner that their mutual political friends, Gale and Ely, wished, for a certain purpose to get some fancy devices made in sugar, and Wengenrath was requested to furnish them. The reply was he had nothing of the kind on hand, and never had sold anything in that line. Britton importuned him from time to time to procure the fancy goods for him. At length as the names of his political friends had been given, the simple-hearted man bought the articles Britton was so anxious to procure, and handed him the same on one of his visits. He would not have taken the trouble to have procured the goods had not the names of Gale, etc., been given. The result was Wengenrath was soon arrested for violating what are known as the Comstock laws. He was tried in Brooklyn, and though the

accused proved an excellent character, and his friends did all they could for him, the laws are so severe that Judge Moore could not do less than impose the lowest prescribed penalty— three months' imprisonment and $150 fine.

Here is another instance of the despicable means which are employed by Comstock and his pliant tool to decoy and induce a good-hearted, unsuspecting person to commit an offense against a vile law he knows nothing about, and then to cause his arrest, trial, and imprisonment for an act he would never have thought of doing had he not been over-persuaded and urged to it by the most villainous intrigue and deception. The unfortunate victim of duplicity, intrigue, and villainy, who was honestly pursuing his honorable, legitimate business, is, at the present writing, in prison serving out the sentence imposed upon him, and Comstock enumerates this case among the desperate cases of obscenity and immorality that he has caused to be brought to justice. Let the reader decide whether Comstock or his victim is the most deserving of imprisonment.

21. CASE OF EDGAR W. JONES.—For several years Mr. Jones has been doing a very active business in Ashland, Mass., supplying thousands of customers by mail with various publications, novelties, and curiosities, embracing prize-packages, "Handbook of Good Manners," "Bashfulness Cured," "How to Make Love," "Parlor Magic," "Tricks with Cards," "Dancing without a Master," "Letter-Writing Made Easy," "Handbook of Business," "Fortune-Teller and Dream Book," "Best Methods of Fishing," "The Art of Ventriloquism," "The Painter's Guide," "The Gem Microscope," etc., with several preparations for the hair, whiskers, etc. In this line of business Mr. Jones built up a trade almost marvelous for the times, filling from 75,000 to 100,000 orders per year. At the time of his arrest, in December, 1877, he had 1,100 reams of paper in his establishment—a four-story building—for his catalogues, circulars, etc., etc., and he gave employment to some sixteen persons in the place, whose duties consisted in folding and stitching catalogues, wrapping goods, filling

envelopes, etc., etc.   He increased the post-office business of
the town immensely.   In the year 1877 he paid over $17,000
for postage stamps alone.

Four years ago he proposed to add to his line of goods
Clark's "Marriage Guide," a work upon physiology, etc., and
principally compiled from "Dunglison's Physiology."   Wishing to proceed carefully, he took a copy to the district
attorney of the U. S. District Court in Boston, for his inspec-
tion and opinion as to its being mailable.   The official looked
it over, and said he could not see why it was not perfectly
proper to send through the mails, and looked upon it as the
same as other medical works.   "There is," said he, "but one
person in the United States who will make you any trouble,
and that is Anthony Comstock of New York.   You had
better send a copy of the work to him, and get his opinion
upon the subject."   Mr. Jones acted upon this advice, and
sent a copy to Comstock, and wrote him asking for his views
upon the subject; but he received no reply; he wrote again,
but no reply was received, when he still wrote again with the
same result.   Then, acting upon the principle that "silence
gives consent," he commenced selling the book, and for four
years sold large numbers of them.

But it seems that Comstock had his evil eyes upon him all
that time, and resolved, when the right time came, to pounce
down upon him as a hawk would alight upon a chicken.   At
the time Comstock caused Jones' arrest, he pronounced his
business fraudulent, and Clarke's work *obscene.*   The matters
complained of were laid before the grand jury, and, upon
looking all his publications over, they could find nothing to
condemn, save it might be a few features in Clarke's "Marriage Guide," which, to their minds, might possibly smack of
obscenity.   Upon this frail tenure they found a bill against
Mr. Jones.

When he found he was indicted, Mr. Jones, of course, was
obliged to procure bail and to look up counsel.   He applied
to Mr. Somerby, who is probably one of the finest lawyers in
Boston, who said: "These obscenity cases are disagreeable

ones, especially in the United States courts. Were the case to be tried in our State courts there would be no trouble in the matter, but in the U. S. courts it is quite a different thing. You can hardly find a first-class lawyer who will defend a case of obscenity in the U. S. courts for a thousand dollars. The best way for you to settle the whole matter up easily is to plead guilty and ask for a light sentence. In that way your fine will be less, and you will get through with the unjust prosecution easier than any other way. It is an outrage on your rights, but the wisest way is to get out of the clutches of the man who has attacked you the best way you can."

Mr. Jones decided to act upon this advice, and when the time of trial came on, he entered a plea of "guilty." The judge, in a short address, used the following language :

"I think there is room to doubt whether this work, Dr. Clarke's 'Marriage Guide,' comes within the statute at all, unless every book on that subject is within the statute ; but after the defendant's plea of guilty, perhaps it must be taken to be a book within the statute. It appears to have been sent to parties having a prurient curiosity, and perhaps his notions in doing this were not very elevated, but the book itself is not immoral or indecent at all, except that it treats of certain subjects supposed to be unknown, or not supposed to be known, and which, I think, ought to be taught in school. I don't see anything at all indecent in the book. I think the allegation in the indictment that the book contained passages which were too indecent to be spread upon the record was made to save the pleader, who wrote the indictment, some trouble, and not for the purpose of not shocking the morals of the court. If it was supposed to be offensive to the court, I am very much obliged to the pleader, but it was *not* so. I think, however, as the plea admits that it is an indecent book, it comes within the statute, but the book treats generally of medical subjects. Upon what examination I have been able to make, I couldn't see that it contains anything indecent. The Government does not claim that it contains anything lascivious, but the book treats of certain things and diseases which are disagreeable, and which, perhaps, young persons should not know, or, as many may think, ought not to know. The defendant, I think, was engaged in a business not very elevating, although he said these books he intended never should be sent to young ladies' schools, yet, as the old or middle-aged people might have a desire to read them, he wished to run as near the line as he could, and, before issuing the book he communicated with the district attorney and Anthony Comstock. As he received no answer from Mr. Comstock, he took silence for assent, and sold the book. However, as he has pleaded that this is an indecent book, I shall sentence him to pay a fine of $150, without costs."

During the proceedings, Mr. Comstock was called to the stand, whereupon he condemned Mr. Jones' business in emphatic terms. Mr. Jones asked him to point out what there was in his business that was vile or immoral. In addition to Clarke's "Marriage Guide," Comstock thought the little book called "Widow's Traps" was a very indecent work and unfit for circulation. Mr. Jones' attorney turned to Mr. Jones and asked him if he had a copy with him. Mr. Jones answered that he had not. At this, Mr. Comstock was still more denunciatory and said the work was suppressed, and that he had seized the plates in New York, and that not a copy of the work was to be had. Jones, knowing that this was wholly untrue, whispered to one of his attendants to go to one of the book-stores in the city and procure a copy. In a few minutes the young man returned with a copy. At this Comstock was evidently taken aback and began to qualify his statements.

Mr. Somerby said: "Mr. Comstock, will you please take that little book and point out such parts as you deem obscene?" Comstock, in a stammering kind of way, said perhaps he was mistaken in the pamphlet, and that possibly there was nothing in it improper. "Did you not say, Mr. Comstock, that you had seized the plates of this book, and that no copies were to be had?" "I think I must have been

wrong; it must have been another work I had in my mind."
"Do you now say, Mr. Comstock, since you see that a copy
of the work has been easily procured, that it is obscene and
unfit for circulation? and, if so, will you point out such parts
and places?" "I do not now think the work is immoral or
obscene." "Mr. Comstock, I consider that you have perjured
yourself right here before the court." The court was evidently of the same opinion; and when Comstock intimated
that the rulings of Judge Benedict of New York would be
materially different from Judge Lowell's, and produced a
long array of written or printed opinions of Benedict, Judge
Lowell told him that he—Judge Lowell—was not governed
by the rulings and decisions of Judge Benedict; that he acted
upon the right of coming to his own decisions, the same as
Judge Benedict undoubtedly did. Comstock was chagrined
at his want of success in the Jones case, and the manner in
which he was looked upon and treated was evidently a matter
of intense disgust to him, and he could not help thinking that
could he have brought the case before Judge Benedict, it
would have terminated differently.

When Mr. Jones was arrested, Comstock went to the post-
office in the village, and stopped all his registered letters and
forbade the cashing of his money orders. He was receiving
from fifty to seventy-five registered letters per day, and when
the trial was over, eleven hundred had accumulated. These
of course he wished to have the benefit of, as any penniless
man would. He had to pay the fine imposed upon him. His
business had been condemned by the court before which he
was brought, and he, very naturally, wished to resume his
regular avocation. To remove the embargo that had been
placed upon his mail, he visited Washington, and had inter-
views with Postmaster-General D. M. Key, and A. A. Bissell,
assistant attorney-general for the Postal Department, but he
was chagrined to find that his visits there could do no good.

He was coolly informed there that Anthony Comstock had
told them that he—Jones—was doing a fraudulent business,
as well as sending out obscene matter, and they could not go

behind Mr. Comstock's information or instructions.   Mr.
Jones called attention to the fact that the grand jury found
nothing wrong in anything he was doing except in Clarke's
"Marriage Guide," and that Judge Lowell had decided that
that was not improper, but ought to be in every family.
"No matter," said Gen. Key, "Mr. Comstock tells us that
you are doing an improper business, and we are bound to
accept his statement."   "But, General Key, is there no proof
I can bring you that will convince you of Comstock's injustice to me ?   The selectmen of my town, every clergyman,
every merchant, and nearly every citizen in the town and
county who knows me, is willing to sign a certificate that I
am doing a legitimate, honest business, and that I am a benefit to the town in which I reside.   I have supplied some
250,000 persons with goods, and not one of them has complained of being defrauded, or that they have not in every
case received the value of their money.   What more must I
do to cause you to decide that my mail ought to be delivered
to me ?"   "All that is of no avail," said Gen. Key; "Mr.
Comstock gives us his word that your business ought to be
suppressed, and we believe his statement.   He is an active
agent in whom we have great confidence.   True, he over-
reaches himself sometimes, but his mistakes are in favor of
the department, and we must stand by him.   He is a good
Christian man, too, and we are bound to take his word in
preference to anybody's else or to all others' combined," or
words to that effect.

Gen. Bissell showed Mr. Jones about two yards of statement from Comstock in reference to Jones' business, but
when the latter asked to read it, he was denied the privilege.
When he desired that it might be read to him, he was again
positively refused.   When he asked to know what statements
and charges it contained, that he might be able to rebut them,
even this request was denied him, and Mr. Jones was strongly
reminded of the old Spanish Inquisition, where a poor victim
was arraigned without knowing who was his accuser or with
what offense he was charged.   There certainly is a similarity.

Mr. Jones returned to this city with a heavy heart, and, upon arriving in New York, proceeded to the office of the mighty Anthony Comstock, who not only rules the entire country, the U. S. Court. the N. Y. Postmaster and officials, publishers, druggists, but even the postmaster-general himself and his attorney.

He thus addressed himself to Mr. Comstock : "Mr. Comstock, you have injured me to the extent of at least $16,000. You have broken up my business. You have stopped my mail. You have taken away my goods and damaged me to a much greater extent than you can ever repair. You have very unnecessarily and very unjustly caused me not only a very heavy loss of property but a great amount of trouble ! Now are you not satisfied ? The Judge of the court before whom I was arraigned has pronounced my business legitimate, everybody who knows me will give me a good name, the hundreds of thousands of persons I have supplied with goods are satisfied with what they obtained of me, nobody has any complaint to make of me but yourself. Can you not let up your heavy hand and let me have my mail matter again and go on with my business, saying to the postmaster-general that you were mistaken as to the character of my business ?" " No," said this modern Torquemada, " I have pronounced you a fraud, and I shall stick to it. You sell a class of goods that are of no benefit to those who purchase them, and you are a swindler. You shall not resume your business again, and if you attempt it I will come down upon you again." In reference to Judge Lowell, Comstock spoke contemptuously and averred that he, Comstock, had not had a fair show in Boston, and that if he had had the case before Judge Benedict in this city, he, Jones, would not have got off in the way he did.

Thus, the man who represents all the morality, all the virtue, all the decency, all the religion in the country, was as obdurate and as unimpressible as a stone. He had set out to crush Mr. Jones, and he was still determined to do it. Mr. Jones was compelled to return to his home and ruined business and to meditate upon the terrible rule of the one-man power with which the country is cursed. The eleven hundred registered letters were returned to the writers, and all he could do was to regret that such a man as Comstock is able to sway such despotic rule in this boasted land of freedom.

Perhaps against no class of victims has Comstock shown more vindictive hatred than against Freethought and Reform publishers.

22. CASE OF E. H. HEYWOOD.—This gentleman is the publisher of a paper called "The Word," at Princeton, Mass. He also publishes a few pamphlets, some upon finance, some upon interest, some upon social philosophy. He is a highly moral man, a gentleman of education and culture, a graduate of Brown University, and one who is highly esteemed by his numerous friends. His views upon marriage, divorce, and kindred subjects differ in many respects from those generally held, but he is entirely honest in his views, and he has the honesty to publish his advanced ideas fearlessly to the world. He has written a pamphlet upon the social question, called "Cupid's Yokes," of which he has sold twenty thousand copies. It is written ably and in unexceptionable language, but as it deals with subjects that are tabooed by orthodoxy, Mr. Comstock made up his mind that Mr. Heywood must be crushed out and sent to prison. He sent a decoy letter from Squan Village, N. J., under the assumed name of E. Edgewell, for a copy each of "Cupid's Yokes" and Trall's "Sexual Physiology," upon the receipt of which he coarsely arrested Mr. Heywood, while in attendance and presiding at a convention at Boston, and hurried him off without allowing him to communicate with his wife or brother who were in the same building.

Mr. Heywood succeeded in giving bail, and his trial before Judge Clark of the United States District Court came off January 17 and 18, 1878. The judge showed a great amount of prejudice against Mr. Heywood, and his rulings partook largely of the intolerance of a Christian bigot. He would not allow Mr. Heywood's witnesses to testify, and his charge was conspicuous for its unfairness and partiality, and was considered by the first lawyers of Boston as a flagrant departure from judicial precedents and from the plainest principles of justice. The case was given to the jury on Friday, the 18th. They were out twenty hours, when the judge, wishing to return to his home in New Hampshire, dismissed the jury till Tuesday, the 22d. The verdict, when rendered, was *guilty*, but altogether a most singular one. The jury said they found him guilty on sending out " Cupid's Yokes," though they did not find the book obscene, within the meaning of the law. It is not strange that such a verdict should excite the risibilities of lawyers and others present. If the book was not obscene, it excited wonder on the part of many how a verdict of guilty could be found.

A motion was at once made by Mr. Heywood's attorney, Mr. Pickering, for a new hearing before two judges with a view of ultimately taking the case before the U. S. Supreme Court at Washington, that the constitutionality of the law may be tested. As, however, that court has recently decided adversely on a lottery case carried up from New York, holding the law to be constitutional, it seems hardly advisable to attempt to get the verdict relative to Mr. Heywood reversed. As these pages are being written, Mr. Heywood is expecting his sentence to be rendered at any time. It is to be hoped that justice and toleration may actuate the judge, and that American liberty may not be outraged by sending Mr. Heywood to prison for uttering his honest convictions and for committing no offense against the laws of morality, truth, or justice. If he is sent to prison for exercising the right of an American citizen it will only be another proof that we still have an Inquisition in this country which denies equal rights and privileges to believers and unbelievers in theological superstitions.

23. CASE OF D. M. BENNETT.—On November 12, 1877, Anthony Comstock, attended by deputy U. S. marshall, Fritz Bernard, visited the office of " The Truth Seeker," and arrested the writer of these pages. In the next issue of his paper, November 17th, appeared the following:

IT HAS COME AT LAST.

One week ago was announced in these columns the arrest in Boston, by Anthony Comstock, of E. H. Heywood, of Princeton, Mass. I was not then aware that the time of my arrest was so near at hand; but at that very moment a warrant had been issued against me, and was only awaiting the pleasure of Mr. Comstock to serve it.

On Monday last, a little after the hour of twelve, while busily engaged in my office, preparing matter for this issue of the paper, that noted champion of Christianity, with a deputy United States marshal at his elbow, visited me with the information that he had a warrant for my arrest. I inquired by what authority and upon what charge? He replied by the authority of the United States and upon the charge of sending obscene and immoral matter through the mails. In reply to my inquiry as to what the objectionable matter was, he exhibited two tracts, one entitled "An Open Letter to Jesus Christ," and the other, "How do Marsupials Propagate their Kind?" He then demanded the amount of those tracts that were on hand, which were delivered to him. He showed a package of tracts, and so forth, which had been put up at this office and sent by mail to S. Bender, Squan Village, N. J., and a registered letter receipt for the money accompanying an order for "The Truth Seeker," tracts, and so forth, which was signed in this office. I asked him whether the party to whom the tracts were addressed was a *real* party, and he had opened his package, or a *bogus* party, and the letter ordering the tracts a mere decoy letter, such as he had used on other occasions. He acknowledged it was the latter, that he had written the order in an assumed name.

Being satisfied that Mr. Comstock was a special agent, empowered by the government of the United States to do the kind of work he is doing, I deemed any show of resistance useless, and passively accompanied him and the deputy marshal to the room of U. S. Commissioner Shields, in the U. S. Court-rooms in the new Post-Office building, who fixed my bail at $1,500, and set Wednesday, the twenty-first, as the day for the preliminary examination. The matter of procuring bail was the next thing in order. Several persons were ready to obligate themselves for my appearance on the day set, but some one owning real estate in the city was required. This was soon procured and I was allowed to go about my business.

Thus I, hard upon sixty years of age, and who for nearly a half-century have been a supporter of our government, am now arrayed by it as an offender against it for sending indecent and blasphemous matter through the mails. The two tracts complained of were published two years ago. The "Open Letter" I wrote, and the other was written by Ex-Rev. A. B. Bradford, as pure and honorable a man as this country can produce, and it is of a purely scientific charac- ter, being originally written for the "Popular Science Monthy." Though the "Open Letter" may be thought pretty radical and outspoken, it is not obscene any more than the notion of a god begetting an offspring upon the person of a young Jewish maiden is obscene ; and I consider that I had a perfectly legitimate right to ask the questions which I did upon the subject. The charge is ostensibly "obscenity," but the real offense is that I presume to utter sentiments and opin- ions in opposition to the views entertained by the Christian Church. Had I been a supporter of the Church and its dogmas, I should not have been disturbed by Comstock though I had sent matter through the mails twice as plain or "indecent"; and so I said to Comstock while on our way to the commissioner's. I asked him why it was, if he was so anxious to prohibit the circulation of obscene literature, that he did not indict the Bible Society. I told him that that book contained more obscenity than any other publication I knew of, and inquired of him where he could find more inde- cent narratives than the account of Abraham and his concu- bine, Lot and his daughters, Jacob and his wives and concu- bines, Judah and Tamar, David and Bathsheba and his other wives, the rape of Amnon upon his sister Tamar, the adultery of Absolom and his father's concubine, of the extensive operations of Solomon with his seven hundred wives and three hundred concubines, and his amorous, lovesick song. He evaded these inquiries by remarking that some ladies near us might hear our remarks, thus virtually confessing that the persons and subjects named were indecent.

I have striven to be a law-abiding, upright citizen, doing injury to none who came within my reach; but I am now in the meshes of the law, held as a criminal, because I have vindicated the freedom of the press and have had the temerity to express my honest convictions. What the result of the trial will be is a question to be decided. Judging by the precedents, it will be likely to go hard with me. I am a prominent advocate of heterodox opinions, and have made myself obnoxious to the theological powers that be, and am considered a belligerent enemy to the system of Christianity. It is desired to remove me as far as possible from the field of action. John A. Lant, prosecuted at the instigation of Comstock, was fined $500 and sentenced to imprisonment at hard labor for eighteen months, and his offense was perhaps no greater than mine. Dr. E. B. Foote, another of Anthony's victims, for simply publishing useful scientific information, was fined $3,500, with costs amounting to $1,500 more. What, then, is there to be expected for D. M. Bennett?

This system of persecution may well be denominated the American Inquisition, and it will be truly lamentable if this great, free government, which was founded upon a non-Christian and anti-theological basis, is to become the head and front of a fearful tyranny. Anthony Comstock, the great informer in these mail cases, is an ardent Christian, and is backed by the Young Men's Christian Association and the God-in-the-Constitution party. He wields an immense power, arresting whom he pleases, and at his beck the United States marshals are prepared to run. The judge presiding over the United States District Court is a firm Christian, and no matter how objectionable or prejudiced he may be thought to be, there is no change of venue; and however severe the verdict or sentence may be, there is no court of appeals to take the case to—no redress. Thus the reader can see at a glance how much like the Spanish Inquisition—before which unfortunate wretches, but two or three centuries ago, were arraigned for opinion's sake—our present system is. The Christian Comstock takes the place of the grand informer, the Christian judge becomes, possibly, the inquisitor-general, Christian jurors become aiders and abettors, and Christian fines and imprisonment take the place of the Cristian rack, wheel, and thumbscrew, beheading-block, and stake. Much progress has been made in the last three hundred years, but much more has yet to be made before a man can express his candid convictions without being in danger of summary arrest and of being deprived of his property and his liberty.

I protest that I have committed no crime. I trust I have wronged no person who walks upon the earth, and if there be supernal beings who float in the ether above the earth, I do not believe that I have wronged them. I have not intended to wrong the smallest child nor the greatest man that lives, and in a court of equal justice I do not fear to meet the consequences of my conduct.

I have not been fighting a personal warfare. I have battled for human rights, for mental liberty and the freedom of the press, and I trust the friends of liberty and equality will not forsake me in my hour of trial. At best, it costs a great deal of money to defend a case in the United States District Court. The best lawyers ask $1,000 to defend a case of "obscenity" before that court, and other expenses are correspondingly heavy. Justice is a very dear article, and then one is liable to be imposed upon in the quality. If a fine is imposed it has to be paid at once or imprisonment follows.

I rest my case with my friends and make no special appeal. I embarked in the Liberal publishing enterprise without capital, and I have held my own. I have no money with which to fee lawyers, to pay fines, nor to meet other heavy expenses. I am willing to spend my last breath in defense of what I believe to be truth, justice, and righteousness, but I have not gold with which to back my feeble efforts to preserve my personal liberty, or to save my life.

I am the Liberal public's most obedient servant,   D. M. B.

When the day arrived for the examination of the editor of "The Truth Seeker," Mr. Comstock seemed to be not quite ready to engage in the examination, and it was deferred for two weeks; and when that time had expired it was put off again. In the meantime "The Truth Seeker" teemed with ardent and sympathetic letters to the persecuted Infidel, and donations to a defense fund came in freely. The examination never came off. An influence was felt from Washington which is believed to have had some effect in this case. Colonel Robert G. Ingersoll wrote the postmaster-general David M. Key, and enclosed the two tracts upon which Mr. Bennett was arrested, and inquired of him if it was the purpose of the Government to prohibit such matter from being sent through the mail. He remarked, if they intended to prosecute cases of that kind that he should defend Bennett, not only in the U. S. Courts, but before the country as well. This letter, or something else, caused the authorities in Washington and in New York to not prosecute the case; and although the grand jury had found a bill against D. M. Bennett, his case was, on the fifth of January, 1878, fully dismissed. Thus, although Comstock had determined that the "old Infidel" should go to prison for the right he had exercised to think for himself and to express his honest convictions, the persecutor was completely foiled; but he still swore, with bated breath, that he would "get the old Infidel into prison," or words to that effect. His will was doubtless good enough, or rather *bad* enough, but for once, at least, his power proved deficient.

24. CASE OF FRANK RIVERS.—This gentleman is a book-seller and publisher in Boston. Not far from January 1, 1878, Comstock arrested him for selling, or sending through the mails, "The Fruits of Philosophy," written more than forty years ago by Dr. Charles Knowlton, and revised by

Charles Bradlaugh and Mrs. Annie Besant. It is the same work which the London Society for the Suppression of Vice, through its agent, Mr. Green, so bitterly prosecuted the latter two persons for selling, causing a sentence of fine and imprisonment to be rendered against them. Mr. Rivers' trial has not been held as these pages are being written, but it cannot well be doubted that Mr. Comstock will do all he can to cause Mr. Rivers to be fined and imprisoned.

Mr. Comstock has displayed an extra amount of zeal in the persecution and prosecution of a class of persons known as *preventionists* and *abortionists*, and has distinguished himself in that particular line. A few of his exploits in this direction will be given:

25. CASE OF EDWARD W. BAXTER.—Mr. Baxter has been a resident of New York about eighteen years, and has been extensively engaged in the furniture trade, but, like many others, became embarassed and failed. Recently he engaged in putting up a remedy for leucorrhœa and other female weaknesses. It was a simple preparation of zinc, and is said to possess excellent qualities. It was advertised in the usual way by means of circulars, etc., and in them a caution is said to be inserted that special care should be taken not to use the remedy after certain exposure has taken place, as its use would almost certainly prevent conception. It is only proper to state in this connection that before embarking in the preparation and sale of the remedy, Mr. Baxter took able legal advice, and the business was pronounced legitimate and lawful; but here was food for Comstock. He ranks prevention of conception as among the greatest crimes in the calendar, and he enjoys no greater pleasure than sending persons to prison and pocketing the fines drawn from them for that crime of immense magnitude.

Comstock sent a decoy letter, obtained one of the circulars, ordered by registered letter some of the remedy, Baxter signed the registered letter receipt, and then he was in the power of the terrible informer, who arrested him at his residence, 993 Sixth avenue, on the evening of Monday, January

7, 1878. He was taken from his family and thrown into
Ludlow Street Jail. On the following day he gave bail in
the sum of $2,500 to await the action of the Grand Jury.
His former partner, Luther P. Tucker, 684 Broadway, was
also arrested and placed in the Tombs prison. Comstock got
out a search warrant and went through his establishment and
found, on an upper floor, goods, circulars, etc., belonging to
Barker & Co., of which firm Baxter is the Co. A bill was
found against Tucker by the Grand Jury.

In connection with this case an important subject is involved
—the sinfulness of preventing conception. The procuring of
abortions cannot be justified by any moral, right-minded
person, but the too rapid increase of population and the
expediency of preventing it by safe and legitimate means is a
question which will demand the serious attention of future
philosophers, physicians, and legislators. There are thousands of children brought into the world that it would be
better for themselves and for the world if they never entered
it. If conception, in these cases, had been prevented, no
wrong would have been committed.

Mr. Baxter had his trial in the U. S. Circuit Court in May,
1878. His lawyer discovered a flaw in the indictment, and
he deemed it best for Baxter to plead guilty and then take
chances for the case to be thrown out of court. He acted
accordingly, and Baxter pleaded guilty, and in a few days
Judge Benedict showed an unusual degree of leniency and
consideration by discharging the prisoner. His joy upon
finding himself a free man once more may be appreciated
when the fact is stated that when Baxter left the court house
and stepped into the street he was fairly delirious, and knew
not at first which way to go, but soon getting his bearings,
he started off on a bee-line for his home, shouting out his
thanks to Judge Benedict and for that flaw in the indictment.

It is indeed a joyful thing to escape the toils of Comstock,
and it is not strange that such a piece of good fortune should
make poor Baxter delirious with joy.

26. CASE OF MADAM RESTELL. — Ann Lohman, usually

known as Madam Restell, who doubtless had for many years been a professional abortionist, was arrested by Comstock in February, 1878. He used in her case the same system of subterfuge, falsehood, and decoying arts that he uses with nearly all his victims. He called upon the Madam at her Fifth avenue mansion, and pretended that his wife or some other female feared she was in an interesting condition, and he wished to procure some medicine that would remove the difficulty. She sold him medicine of some kind calculated to remove obstructions. He visited her the second time to make some additional purchases, on which occasion he arrested her and took her to the Tombs, where she was placed under $5,000 bail, and not finding it easy to obtain, she was detained a prisoner.

It is believed that a prominent object which Comstock had in view in arresting this woman was to obtain some of the wealth which she possessed in abundance. The treasury of his "Society for the Suppression of Vice" had become exhausted. The donations of the previous year had not been as generous as in other years, and it began to be a matter of some solicitude with him as to where the money was to come from to admit of his drawing his annual salary of four thousand dollars. It was believed that if two or three indictments could be obtained against that wealthy woman, who had obtained her money in so questionable a manner, large sums could be drawn from her in the name of decency, morality, and religion.

The Madam was past sixty years of age; she had lived a quiet and unobtrusive life for more than thirty years, and the annoyances and anxieties of being prosecuted by Anthony Comstock upon the charge of aiding in procuring abortion preyed upon her mind excessively. As before remarked, no person who has not experienced the anxiety of mind and the feeling of disgrace attendant upon an arrest by Comstock, upon such charges as he prefers, can realize the utter wretchedness which such an arrest produces. There is nothing in the world like it for making one feel forsaken and booked for a term of prison life. Madam Restell experienced this feeling to the full. She knew that, although her services had saved from disgrace many wealthy aristocratic families belonging to the most fashionable churches, public sentiment was aroused against her, and that the medical fraternity wished her removal from the lucrative position she occupied, and it was doubtless to subserve their interests in part that Comstock commenced his persecuting operations against her. She experienced much difficulty in obtaining acceptable bail. Many persons of wealth would have readily signed her bail bond could they have done so without the publicity that would necessarily attend it and the odium attached to being security for a person arrested upon such a charge. Her bail cost her not a little money, and one or more of the bondsmen procured at considerable expense surrendered her, and she was forced to look up other bail.

The anxieties and troubles connected with the situation, with the probable conviction, imprisonment, and heavy fine that would attend the approaching trial, preyed upon the unhappy woman's mind until she was driven nearly to insanity. On the first of April she was to appear before Judge Donahue, when an examination of her case would take place. She dreaded the day with a dread almost inconceivable, and early on the morning of that day, and while it was yet night, supposed to be about two o'clock A. M., she left her bed and repaired to her bath-room, when with a large carving-knife from the kitchen, and while reclining in the bath, she cut her throat from ear to ear, and there cold and dead she was found by her domestics in the morning. It was a shocking affair, but she had placed herself beyond Comstock's reach and rendered it impossible for him to clutch any of her money. It was doubtless a heavy disappointment to that Christian official.

According to the statement which Comstock himself made to a mutual friend, this was the fifteenth case where he had driven his victims to suicide, and to this number a larger list could probably be added of those who by his persecutions and prosecutions, with the imprisonments and attendant disgrace and wretchedness, have been driven to an untimely grave, as effectually and with far greater mental suffering than if he had assassinated them with knife or pistol. What a reflection must it be to a man, with human feelings in his breast, that he has caused the death of more than thirty persons and the despoiling of his unfortunate victims of hundreds upon hundreds of thousands of dollars! But such is the power of Christian persecution—of the American Inquisition—at the present day.

After the sad taking off of Madam Restell the papers of the city and country were somewhat severe in their comments in reference to Comstock and his system of inveigling and decoying persons into his power to crush and destroy them. "The Daily Graphic" contained the following:

"Is it right to do evil that good may come? Is it a good thing for the community at large in putting down one form of vice to permit and encourage the development of another? Is not there danger in any method of ridding the world of one class of social parasites which develops another? . .

"Not only is "the suppressor gratified by finding his vice," but he carefully cultivates its growth. In order that he may get the credit which follows energy and success, he selects some person that he thinks has committed the crime which it is his duty to detect, a duty on which his bread and butter depends, and he goes to the person, and by all the inducements which human ingenuity can suggest he urges and beseeches him to commit the crime so that he can get the reward. . . . .

"The man becomes the detective and informer, and ceases to be the public-spirited citizen.

"In the present case, if Mr. Comstock has been correctly reported, he did not originally take up the Restell matter because he thought it a public duty to do so. No one had complained of the woman for prosecuting her nefarious business, and it is current rumor that the pills and powders which she sold were a harmless sham, and that she herself was simply a fraud, whatever might have been the intention of herself or her patrons. Mr. Comstock was badgered into entrapping Restell. Men said to him: 'Yes, you are afraid of big game. You arrest the poor, but you permit one of the rich women of New York to prosecute her trade openly in this city.' With the woman or her trade no one can have any sympathy, and very few will regret her end. Mme. Restell is nothing, but the good of society is of the highest importance. The development of a class of spies and detectives whose fortune and fame would depend upon their success in entrapping the members of society into the commission of crime would threaten the very existence of society. The detective has a tremendous advantage over any private individual. He has the sympathies of society on his side. His methods are condoned so long as his motives are right, and his motives are taken for granted in nine cases out of ten. If, on the other hand, we look at the history of the detective service in this city we see how little deserving detectives have been of any credit. The whole detective service has been rotten, and there is hardly a question that if the truth were known detective and thief were synonymous in most cases.

"Let us not forget then that there are great dangers lurking in our present methods of suppressing immorality. We may produce a class of professional liars, informers, and decoys. And if we do, it will be pretty certain that we will not suppress vice, but suppress those who do not 'come down' to the informer. As yet we are safe, but the present system needs careful watching lest it should become the nursing mother of a class of rotten detectives."

After a full account of the Madam's funeral, the "Telegram" gave the following report of a conversation that took place at the Madam's house: Mr. Farrell, a son-in-law of the Madam, stated that she had at one time intended to flee to Canada; but she gave up this plan at the persuasion of her friends. He then went on to say: "Comstock's attempt to make her appear the vile person he represented her was an outrage, and his coming here with six officers expecting to find a house full of patients must have been a great disappointment to him, as it only ended in the arrest of one old woman. There never has been a patient taken in this house, and all attempts to prove it would have failed."

The "Herald," in a report of a sermon by the Rev. Charles McCarthy, contained the following: "In my opinion, in the manner in which she was entrapped, she was more sinned against than sinning. The fraud and falsehood by which she was made amenable to a law that is universally violated by the medical profession of this city cannot be too strongly condemned. When, in the Great Assize, the question is asked, By what means was this misguided woman driven in her old age to self-slaughter? and the answer is given, She was hunted down by miserable subterfuge, by cunning and heartless fabrications, by open and mean lying, and by specious arguments which were craftily devised to work upon her better nature, what will the judge of all the earth say to this pretended suppression of vice and crime by means in themselves the most appropriate to promote vice and crime? This strange tragedy is calculated to call attention not only to the degrading methods by which crime is detected, but also to that condition of social degradation which fosters the crime, while in a few isolated cases it seeks to punish the criminal."

As great as the crimes of Madam Restell were, they were not to be compared to those against human rights and personal liberty committed by Anthony Comstock.

27. CASE OF DR. SARA B. CHASE.—"The Truth Seeker" for May 18, 1878, contained the following account of the arrest of that lady:

"*More Comstockism.*—On the ninth inst., Anthony Comstock, attended by his accomplice and partner, Joseph A. Britton, and officer James G. Howe, visited the house of Dr. Sara B. Chase, No. 56 West Thirty-third street, and arrested that lady and took her before Judge Morgan at the Tombs, where she was held in $1,500 bail upon the enormous charge of having sold two female syringes, gotten up expressly for cleansing and healthful purposes.

"Dr. Sara B. Chase has resided in this city nearly four years, and has become well known as a lecturer on physiological subjects before separate classes of ladies and gentlemen, and also as a successful practitioner in homeopathic medicine. She has recently started 'The Physiologist,' an excellent reform and health monthly, of which she is editor and publisher.

"She has given several courses of lectures in Brooklyn, and that is the home of Anthony Comstock. It seems that not long since he opened a correspondence with the lady, upon the subject of procuring a syringe from her. He did not write in his own name, but followed, rather, the course for which he has become notorious, of writing over a fictitious name. He this time personated a Mrs. Farnsworth, who had attended Mrs. Chase's lectures and had received valuable information thereby, and wished to procure a syringe from her, but on account of illness was unable to be present on the occasion of the doctor's last lecture in Brooklyn, and she would send her husband to the doctor's residence for one of the instruments. In fact, Comstock himself took this letter to the lady, and passed himself off as the veritable Mr. Farnsworth whose wife wanted a syringe. He received the instrument, with full directions as to how it should be used. He was so well pleased with it that, on the following day, he took his bosom friend, Joseph A. Britton, to see the doctor and procure one of those valuable instruments for his wife.

"Dr. Chase being, of course, willing to sell these valuable syringes to every married lady who wished them, cheerfully sold one to the honorable Mr. Britton; and then it was that the pure and spotless Mr. Anthony Comstock made himself known, telling the lady that he was himself no less than Anthony Comstock, and that she must accompany him to the Tombs. Before leaving the premises, however, he caused the house to be searched and overhauled in a most shameless manner. He caused the ladies of the family to be shut up in a room, and then every room, closet, drawer, and every conceivable place was examined, even to bundles of letters and correspondence. He continued the search until, in the pocket of one of the lady's dresses, hanging in a closet, he found the decoy letter he had written in the name of Mrs. Farnsworth, which he carefully took with him, that the proofs of his lying and villainy might not easily be produced against him.

"As an instance of Comstock's meanness, it may be stated that among the lady's private papers he found an article on 'Fœticide,' which was decidedly against the practice of it; but, in order to present her case as unfavorably as possible, in the statement which he furnished 'The Tribune,' he mentioned finding the article, but changed the title to 'Fœticide — *When it should be done.*' There were no grounds for his making that change ; and a man who would do such a deed would probably commit forgery or theft.

"In the same 'Tribune' article, Comstock exhibited more of the ignoble traits of his character by attempting to prejudge the case in the public mind by placing the lady at a disadvantage by styling her a rival of Madam Restell, and making ungentlemanly and uncalled-for remarks about her mouth. On the way to the Tombs, Comstock spoke to the lady about her paper, 'The Physiologist,' and said he regarded it as an immoral paper and one that ought not to be allowed circulation. She found no trouble in giving bail, and thus the Christian Comstock was cheated out of the pleasure of causing her to be kept in the Tombs over night.

"The crime which the agent of the Society for the Suppression of Vice charges against Mrs. Chase, is that by the syringes which she recommends and sells, she places it in the power of wives to prevent conception. This he holds to be very criminal in any one whom he chooses to make his victim, but when the president of his society, Mr. Samuel Colgate, wishes to engage in the business of selling an article which he recommends as a preventive of conception, he does not interfere in the enterprise and does not try to bring his friend Colgate to justice, and in this laudable clemency he is seconded by the amiable United States district-attorney, Mr Stewart L. Woodford, who knows how Mr. Colgate has violated the law, but, himself being an honored member of the Society for the Suppression of Vice, refuses to prosecute its honored but intolerant president. It is of course very criminal in Dr. Chase to take any means to provide persons with the means for preventing conception, but Mr. Colgate may sell tons of vaseline, which, blended with salicylic acid, he recommends as being potent in preventing conception or removing the effects of it, and he shall not be disturbed. He is a pious man, he supports the Church, he loves Jesus and hates Freethinkers—and he is at liberty to sell all the vaseline he wishes. No laws nor courts nor Comstocks shall be sufficient to interfere with him in his lucrative career. Being a "truly good man," he is to be allowed uninterruptedly the privileges which belong only to the faithful. He may do as he pleases sitting under his own vine and fig-tree, and none shall make him afraid.

"This question of preventing conception is one which is bound to be discussed and passed upon by the American public as it has been by the people of Great Britain. It will be canvassed in all its aspects, and it will be examined into with a view to decide whether it is criminal or not. To all intents and purposes this is an open question, and must remain so for some time to come. Anthony Comstock, seconded by the members of Congress and of our State Legislature, has attempted to close it, and to pronounce prevention as criminal, but it is very doubtful if his dictum will stand through all coming time. It is at all events our privilege and our pleasure to examine the subject carefully.

"There are cases where the prevention of conception is not only harmless but entirely proper. Suppose a mother has ten children already, with one at the breast, is it absolutely sinful to take harmless measures that the number be not increased? Suppose a pair in great poverty with a house full of children half-clad and half-fed, the anxious parents driven to the greatest straits to be able to supply even this half-allowance, ought they to be sent to the penitentiary for using prudential means to stop the increase of their half-fed and half-clothed offspring? If one or both parents have the seeds of consumption in them, if three of their children have already fallen victims to pulmonary diseases, and two others are hastening on in the same road, is it wrong for them to use laudable means to prevent still others being added to this woeful number? If the father is eaten up with syphilis, or is semi-rotten with scrofula, is it sinful for the mother by a cleansing process to use such a simple preventive as will not increase the number of children to be miserable heirs to disease and wretchedness? If the father has by a long course of dissipation brought upon himself imbecility or semi-idiocy, shall the mother not be allowed to prevent an unsound mental and physical offspring to be born to such a father? If the tendency to insanity is strong in the husband's family, if his father and grandfather became hopelessly insane, and in a fit of madness butchered their wives and children, is it positively criminal for the mother to use an ablution of water applied by the use of a female syringe to prevent the miserable, dangerous stock from being perpetuated? If a mother by toil and child-bearing is broken down in health and strength until she is hardly able to drag herself around, and if in her last confinement she suffered to the extent that her life was despaired of, and her nearest friends believed she could not survive, and could not possibly pass through another such ordeal, would she be committing a crime against God or man by using a simple means of prevention? Are there not thousands upon thousands of similar cases where prevention is not in the slightest sense wrong, but in the highest degree commendable and proper? and shall Anthony Comstock and his legal abettors send people to prison for aiding this thing? In fact, is it not right for any wife or mother to decide for herself whether she wishes to bear more children or not? Take China, for instance, where parts of that country are excessively overcrowded, where hundreds of thousands are starving to death for the want of food, and where dead children are offered in the market as food, is it criminal to prevent by sensible means the birth of more children under such circumstances? Is it not better, far better, that conception be prevented than that children be born into the world to die of starvation or to be eaten up by the vilest diseases?

"In any case of prevention that may be used, even admitting that it is a crime, it is most difficult to know whether the crime has absolutely been committed, for it is impossible to be told whether conception would have taken place or not. The proportion of conceptions to the possibilities is extremely small. It is probable the proportion is much the same as with the seeds of trees of the forest, the herbs of the field, or the ova of the fishes of the sea—perhaps not one in a thousand produces its like. We have seen no estimate by physiologists as to what the proportion is, but probably it is not more than one to fifty or to one hundred; hence it must be seen that if the most effectual preventive is employed that can be devised, it must be highly improbable that a crime has been committed. The most effectual preventive known in the world (and we hope Comstock will not cause our arrest for making it known) is for the sexes to *strictly remain apart;* and of course, then, this is the most criminal of all the modes, and persons guilty of it should be sent to prison for not less than ninety-nine years.

"This question has attracted the earnest attention of some of the best men and the deepest thinkers in England, and the subject is bound to arouse attention in our own country. There are some persons depraved enough to think it would be better to place some check upon the too great evils of over-population, rather than too see the distress repeated here that exists in China, in India, and in some of the over-crowded cities of Europe. Those persons do not regard with favor the introduction of miserable children into this world, whose parents are only fitted to bring a helpless or diseased offspring into existence, and, with Darwin, they think that in the propagation of no domestic animals are men so careless as with their own race. In discussing this important subject Darwin says: "Excepting in the case of man himself hardly any ne is so ignorant as to allow his worst animals to breed."

The class of intelligent persons referred to do not regard the sexual part of the human organization as being wholly vile, all knowledge of which is positively criminal and must needs be suppressed. On the other hand, they hold that the organs which constitute us men and women are as honorable, and should be as well understood, as any other parts of our bodies, and that it is not criminal to understand their uses and proper needs. It is only Anthony Comstock and such prurient minds as his that see so much that is vile and criminal in the distinguishing features that make us men and women. It is such as he who think that people ought to be sent to prison for even looking at the picture of a nude human being; and it remains to be tested whether Comstock shall be the permanent law-maker and dictator in our miscalled free country.

"The subject, as observed, of population and over-population is of vital importance to the human race, present and future; it cannot be ignored, and should not be. This subject must come to the front; it must be examined; it must for some time in the future remain an open question; and we decidedly hold that neither Anthony Comstock nor his pet members of Congress and of the Legislature have any right to close it.

"The most villainous of Comstock's tricks in this business is the effort to represent Mrs. Chase as an abortionist, when nothing is further from the truth. No person feels more against that crime or has spoken more strongly against it than has the lady herself. Comstock will not be able to prove anything of that kind against her, and it is only by his despicable course in putting false headings to his 'Tribune' articles that he can accomplish his vile purposes. It is not enough to bring odium upon the lady by causing her arrest, but he seems determined to prejudice her case all he can in the public mind before it comes to trial. If such a man can be a good man, where, pray, are the evil ones to be found?

"Is it, indeed, so great a crime to sell a female syringe that people must have their business broken up, their reputation blasted for it for life? If it is a crime for Dr. Chase to sell a syringe of this kind, every druggist in the country ought to be sent to prison for life. There is probably not a druggist in the United States who has not sold female syringes. We were in the drug business a quarter of a century, and we sold many scores of them, and did not dream that we were committing a crime by doing so. From what we know of the importance of cleanliness in maintaining the health of both sexes, we are fully convinced that these syringes should be used much more than they are. We are decidedly of the opinion that no lady's toilet is complete who has not one of them. Those who lack them are not in possession of a necessary aid to cleanliness and health. A person who supplies ladies with them is really doing a good deed to his fellow-beings. In preventing their diffusion and making it a crime, Anthony Comstock is again proving himself an enemy to his race."

It is a cause of pleasure that when Comstock presented the case of Dr. Chase before the grand jury, they failed to see that the lady had committed any offense for which she ought to be punished or that she had violated any law of the land. One of the grand jury asked Comstock if it was his intention to drive Dr. Chase to suicide as he had driven Madam Restell. The agent for the Y. M. C. A. and for the Society for the Suppression of Vice evidently felt chagrined at his want of success in this case, and the congratulations extended towards Dr. Chase were hearty and numerous. Many of the papers condemned Comstock's course. An indignation meeting was held in Science Hall, Saturday evening, May 25th, in which Dr. Chase gave the opening address, and was followed by G. L. Henderson and J. D. McClelland, attorney. The latter, being thoroughly acquainted with Comstock's manner of doing business, was able to speak to the point. He gave several facts within his own knowledge connected with the Comstock cases he had defended. One case in particular is worthy of attention. It was of a man whom Comstock had arrested for sending—in answer to a decoy letter from Comstock—a syringe through the mail. The unfortunate man was thrown into prison, and his wife and children left to suffer. On the trial, despite the hard swearing of Comstock, and the severe rulings of Judge Benedict, he succeeded in causing the jury to stand six and six. He proved, by several eminent physicians of the city, that the syringe was a valuable one and innocent of any harm. This amounted to nothing with Judge Benedict. The speaker pronounced the rulings of Judge Benedict—from whose court there was then no appeal—as being of a very severe character. He expressed his joy that the law was now changed, so that there is a chance for a case to be opened and appealed; and, if justice demands it, a new hearing can be had.

After the jury had thus disagreed, a new trial was obtained, and the second time he succeeded in dividing the jury six to six. Even for the third time this result was produced; but on the fourth trial the rulings of the judge were so severe upon the prisoner that a verdict was secured, and the unfortunate prisoner was declared guilty, and he was sentenced to two years' imprisonment for the trivial offense of sending a syringe through the mail.

When the husband had thus been sent to prison, the young wife saw very hard times. She could get work but a portion of the time, and to keep herself and children from starvation she was compelled to pawn one article of jewelry after another, and one keepsake after another, and by this course alone was she able to keep herself and children alive; but at length everything of any value that could be pawned was put in pledge, and there was nothing but utter want to stare her in the face. A few months after this the attorney one morning saw this woman arraigned as a lawless prostitute before the police court. He sought an opportunity to speak to the wretched woman, and he asked her how in the world she had come down to occupy that position. With tears in her eyes she told him she had struggled to obtain bread for her children as long as she possibly could, and when everything was gone, and she was upon the point of starvation, she had yielded to the importunities of her landlord, and had prostituted her body to save the lives of her children, and that she had since gone down step by step till she was where she was. "Ah!" said the attorney, "if there is a God, if there is a future world of retributive justice, if there is a place of torment, that man, Anthony Comstock, will there have to answer for the human wreck and suffering he has produced!"

He further stated that the cases of conviction that Comstock proudly boasted of had cost the hottest tears of anguish and the keenest pangs of sorrow known to the human heart, and that the same had been accomplished by the vilest arts of the informer, the basest falsehood, the most despicable tricks of the decoyer, as well as by treachery of the blackest kind. "More than that," he asserted, "Comstock and his accomplice have been guilty of perjury in prosecuting the hapless victims whom they have thrust into prison." He believed Anthony Comstock to be one of the worst men he ever knew —one who was utterly lost to every feeling of pity and compassion. The manner in which he pictured the heartless villain stood out in bold relief before the vision of the audience present.

As these pages are being written, Dr. Chase is about commencing a suit for damages against Comstock for false imprisonment and for injuries she has sustained in her business. At the time of her arrest her house was full of paying tenants, her lectures were well attended, and she had a remunerative practice, but the odium connected with an arrest by Comstock, and upon such a charge is sufficient to drive away large numbers of timid people who are afraid to have the least connection with a suspected person. Her business has suffered excessively, and it is to be hoped she may be able to recover suitable damages. And it would seem but simple justice that the society which employs him and pays him $4,000 per year for the contemptible services he renders should be made to pay for the needless wretchedness, misery, and loss of property they cause. If a man or a company keep a vicious dog which attacks and tears people to pieces, they ought to be responsible for his conduct. It is to be hoped Dr. Chase may be successful in her suit.

Too much space is perhaps being occupied with this character, far more than is due him, but it is desirable to make a fair exhibit of the kind of work he is doing in the name of decency, morality, and the Christian religion. As the recognized agent and executor of the very Christian Society for the Suppression of Vice and the Y. M. C. A., and as a striking type of the latest form of Christian persecutions, it is but proper that a due amount of space in this work be accorded him. Less than thirty of his cases have here been given, being not one-tenth of the whole number of which he boasts. Had the nearly three hundred arrests he has made been given in detail, with all the anxiety, trouble, personal inconvenience and wretchedness they have caused, they would doubtless fill a volume as large as this. Probably enough has been given to enable the reader to obtain a pretty clear view of the character of the man. But lest all his Christian qualities may not be appreciated, one or two additional instances of his devotion to decency and high orthodox morals are given.

In the issue of the "Waverly Magazine" for November 10, 1877, appeared an advertisement reading like this: "To SPORTS.—An elegant book for you will be sent on receipt of fifty cents. Address J. G. Phillips, Box 49, Squan Village, N. J." This was pointed out to the writer as being the work of Comstock, and that it was he who was doing that advertising. It was known at once that it was one of his post-offices, that he had a home in that vicinity, and that he had sent to the writer at least two letters from that point under the name of S. Bender (probably the father of Miss Ella), ordering "The Truth Seeker," the "Open Letter to Jesus Christ," the "Marsupial" tract, and several others, as well as a copy of Dr. Trall's "Sexual Physiology." It was from Squan Village, under the same name, that he ordered goods from E. W. Jones, and it was from Squan Village that he wrote to E. H. Heywood for "Cupid's Yokes" and another copy of Trall's "Physiology." It was from Squan Village that the interesting letters came forth to the impressible Dr. Morrison.

It was easy to reach the conclusion that J. G. Phillips, S. Bender, Miss Ella Bender, and Anthony Comstock were one and the same person. A friend ordered a copy of Anthony's "Book for Sports," inclosing fifty cents in a letter which he had registered. In due time the receipt came back signed "J. G. Phillips," and after a few days came a copy of a cheap London edition of the New Testament, which in England retails at twopence, and of which hundreds of thousands are given away. In quantities they probably cost two cents. On a corner of the wrapper was a small gum label, reading, "From the American Tract Society, 150 Nassau street, New York," which place, by the by, is where Comstock has his headquarters. Here the connection between J. G. Phillips of Squan Village and Anthony Comstock of 150 Nassau street was thoroughly established. But it was thought his profits were too large. For the fifty cents a book had been received which cost at the most three cents, postage two cents. Fifty cents for what cost five is a thousand per cent, which in hard times is a very large profit. In a few days, however, came back the fifty cents in a registered letter, with a pious homily which bore no signature; but it could have been from none else than the Squan Village firm.

At this stage of the business the party ordering thought he was a Testament ahead. He had received a copy of that esteemed book, a pious letter, and his money back again—a very good investment. It could not easily be seen where Comstock could make much by doing business in that way, for he had used seventeen cents in postage stamps besides the stationery. His game was better understood a few days later when there came from the same source in a sealed envelope with six cents in stamps upon it, some fifteen or twenty pages from a most villainously, obscene book entitled, "Pleasing Memoirs," with an indecent, obscene picture of the most objectionable character. The envelope was directed in a disguised hand.

That all this was the work of the Christian Comstock there cannot be the slightest doubt. An intelligent person went to Squan Village to interview the postmaster and others, and he learned that J. G. Phillips, S. Bender, and Anthony Comstock are the same person, and that the postmaster there was privy to the artful games Comstock had been playing. The name and address given by the person who ordered the "Book for Sports" to J. G. Phillips were never given to any other person, so all that came to that address must have come from the party who had the name and address. It could not have been otherwise. It was Comstock and nobody else that mailed that vile stuff. He was the only one who had the address referred to, and he was the only one who had that kind of literature, having monopolized all there is in the country. In the whole transaction it is easy to trace his low cunning and his diabolic desire to catch some unsuspecting, unsophisticated person in his snares. Let others decide whether such a man is fit to control the morals of the country, and to be entrusted with unlimited power to persecute, to imprison, and to take the property and life of those far better than himself.

The latest instance of Comstock's Christian morality and purity is as follows: On the night of June 14, 1878, Anthony Comstock, attended by five other men, supposed to be brother members of the Society for the Suppression of Vice, went to a house of prostitution, 224 Greene street, and those six godly men induced three frail women, who make their bread by the prostitution of their bodies, for the consideration of fourteen dollars, to lay off all their wearing apparel, and, in a closed room, to expose their persons, like so many original Eves, to the six men aforesaid. After these young Christian Associates had feasted their eyes to the full, and even Comstock had become satisfied, he then assumed his dignity of office and said they were his prisoners, and that he was Anthony Comstock. He drew a revolver, and pointing it at the woman who kept the house, declared, in the most imperious manner, that if she stirred he would blow her brains out. He ordered them to wrap blankets around them and to march off to prison just as they were, but he finally relented enough to let them put their garments on, and they, with the landlady, were marched to the fourteenth ward station and kept in prison several days, when they succeeded, at an expense of three hundred dollars each, in obtaining bail. In the excitement of the occasion the landlady lost a seventy-five-dollar diamond ring from her finger, but she was hurried out of the room before she could have time to find it. It is thought that one of the six good men were enriched by finding that valuable piece of jewelry, as the landlady has not seen it since. Is it to be supposed that the Young Men's Christian Association and the Society for the Suppression of Vice will be proud of this last moral act of their agent and representative? Was ever a baser, lower, and more contemptible act ever committed by a man? Can any state of things justify such a dirty, indecent piece of business? Were not the poor unfortunates, who are reduced to such pitiful expedients to earn their daily bread, quite as honorable as Comstock?

Comstock has frequently asserted, in the public press and in private conversation, that he makes no arrests and enters upon no case until he has received authority to do so from his society, or the committee of the society, having such business in charge. If that is so, his Society for the Suppression of Vice must be held responsible for this filthy piece of business in that house of prostitution. That Christian society is either *particeps criminis* in the disgusting affair or their secretary and agent has lied. At all events, they cannot evade the official acts of their agent and representative.

Almost every man in the world, whether good or bad, may be said to have had in the past his archetype, prototype, or precursor, from whom he has patterned or from whom he has seemed to take qualities and characteristics to govern his own conduct. In looking for such an antitype for Anthony Comstock among the violent and cruel persecutors which the Christian Church has raised up, the mind almost intuitively reverts to Torquemada, the demoniac inquisitor-general of Spain, for a sketch of whose career the reader is referred to page 508. It may well be conceded that Comstock would have made a very vigilant inquisitor-general, and that he would have delighted in arresting, toruring, and burning heretics and every person who presumed to differ from the standard of thought and opinion to which he pays allegiance. Though Torquemada caused the death of one hundred thousand innocent persons, and subjected a greater number to cruel torture and imprisonment, he was too pure a man, too honest and sincere, to stand as a fit type for Anthony Comstock, for he did not follow his infernal system of per secution for the purpose of making money by the sufferings of his victims as Comstock has done. A farther search must be made for a prototype. O, here is one, it is Matthew Hopkins, the notorious witchfinder of the seventeenth century, some account of whom may be found on page 796. There are some striking points of resemblance between the two men. Hopkins was a witchfinder-general in the seventeenth century as Comstock is obscenity-finder-general in the nineteenth century. Hopkins was clothed with a species of legal authority to prowl over several of the shires of England, seizing his victims wherever he could find them, and Comstock has been clothed with a similar sort of legal authority to prowl over some of these American States, hunting down his unfortunate victims in the same kind of way. It was the pleasure of Hopkins to seize upon those he or others declared to be witches and to put them through the most fiendish tests and to bring them to torture and death. Comstock eagerly siezes upon his victims, whom he accuses of obscenity or immorality or heterodoxy with equal venom, hate, and cruelty, considering the age of the world in which he lives, and from this view he has probably caused an equal number of deaths. It has been observed that Comstock has boasted of causing fifteen persons to commit suicide, and it is probable that others who have been forced to an involuntary death by means of his heartless persecutions are not fewer in number; and those whose hearts he has torn with anguish and deep grief, as with hooks of steel, are to be numbered by scores and hundreds. Matthew Hopkins never gloated over his victims more with the hate of a demon than Comstock has gloated over his. Both prosecuted their diabolical business in the name of decency and morality, and both were arrant hypocrites.

It will be remembered that Hopkins pursued his operations in this manner: When an unfortunate woman was complained of to him as a witch, or of whom it was even suspected that she was a witch, he at once shut her in a room, stripped her naked, and placed her in a very painful position, which, if she did not retain, he bound her with strong cords, and kept her thus without food, drink, or sleep for twenty-four hours. When exhausted nature yielded to the demand for sleep he roused her and made her walk till her feet were blistered; and when, by this Christian treatment, he had reduced his victim to a state of insanity or imbecility, he made her confess to having had intercourse with the devil, and with having given birth to imps in the forms of lizards, toads, snakes, and goats, whose father was the devil; and then, upon that enforced confession, he caused her to be tortured and to be put to death in the most shocking manner.

Comstock has exhibited similar traits of character. He is equally merciless and equally callous to every sentiment of human kindness. The victims of Hopkins were largely females, while those of Comstock are divided between the sexes, and those he has succeeded in making sufficiently wretched for any purpose. Every man whose arrest he has caused had a wife, a mother, or a sister to be rendered heart-broken by the deep disgrace cast upon them and the great wrong thus inflicted.

A favorite way, it will be remembered, that Hopkins had for testing his unfortunate victims was by "the swimming process." The miserable wretch was tied up in a sheet and thrown upon the surface of a pond or river. If she sunk and was drowned she was supposed to be innocent, but she was drowned, nevertheless; but if she floated, as about nine in ten did, then she was declared a witch, and was either dragged through ponds and ditches until life was extinct, or she was hanged or burned, as the decision might be.

But finally the people became so incensed at Hopkins' cruelty that they concluded to try his own test upon him. They tied him in a sheet and threw him upon the water, and he floated; hence he was declared a witch or wizard, and he was accordingly executed upon the spot. If the analogy is carried out in Comstock's case, there are many who, having a most bitter recollection in connection with him, will not be sorry. It is believed by many that his days of usefulness are over, and that he ought to be allowed to depart in peace.

In one respect Hopkins was far superior to Comstock; Hopkins was not guilty of the meanness of decoying and entrapping his victims by duplicity, intrigue, and lies, that he might have the pleasure of torturing them. He waited for others to enter a complaint, and did not sneak around as a spy, and lie in wait for those whom he wished to subject to his power. It would be well were Anthony Comstock as honorable a man as was Matthew Hopkins.

A few additional quotations from the press, bearing upon Comstock's manner of conducting his business, may not be inappropriate here. The Philadelphia "Record" spoke as follows:

"Mr. Comstock has been trying to trap unwary sinners by forging letters and buying forbidden wares. It strikes us as bad policy to use as instruments for reforming offenders men who are meaner than the offenders themselves. People judge a cause by the character of its advocates, and principles by their exponents; and the cause of morality must suffer seriously when such men as Comstock publicly espouse it and become known as its ministers. He is meaner by a few degrees than the agents of our Society for the Prevention of Cruelty to Animals, and this is saying much against Comstock, but we have his own confession in proof of our assertion. He is a self-convicted sneak and hypocrite, without moral honor, and must naturally do the cause of morality far more harm than good."

Bonner's "New York Ledger" in connection with the arrest of Dr. Sara B. Chase, said:

"*Is Deception Justifiable?*—Our sympathies are with Anthony Comstock, or any one else, in every proper effort which can be made to punish the parties who deal in prohibited arti cles; but if the following extract from a report in the 'Tribune' be true, we think Mr. Comstock acted in, to say the least, a very questionable manner in the instance referred to:

"The 'Tribune' states that on Tuesday Mr. Comstock went to the house of Mrs. Chase, ostensibly to buy an article she was forbidden by law to sell—having previously bought one of the same kind. *He told her he wanted to make the purchase for a friend.* 'Her face,' continues the report, 'lighted up at once, and she turned about promptly and led the way to her office '—where she was arrested.

"Is there any necessity for practicing such deceit, in order to arrest a person engaged in a nefarious business? We think not. At any rate, we should think an honorable, high-toned man would find it difficult to reconcile with his own feelings of self-respect the resorting to such measures, even on account of their supposed necessity in the abatement of a great evil."

Oliver Johnson's "Orange Journal" (N. J.) contained the following:

"Mr. Anthony Comstock is entitled to the thanks of every lover of social purity for his efforts to suppress the traffic in obscene literature and to expose the murderers of unborn children. In this work the more skillful his devices, the heavier his hand, the better. But he should have a care lest his persecutions of the guilty degenerate into persecutions of the innocent. There are honest differences of opinion among men upon some very important and delicate physiological questions, and it is not for Mr. Comstock to make himself a *doctrinaire*, to suppress by violence the right of speech and of printing upon such subjects. He must remember that it is possible for very good people to hold opinions contrary to his own, and contrary even to those generally held in the community, upon physiological subjects; and if he would retain the good will of the community he should learn how to discriminate between the agents and abettors of impurity, and well-meaning people, however mistaken, who are laboring, according to their best light, to promote the public welfare."

Colonel Robert G. Ingersoll expressed his opinion of Comstock in these words, "I regard Comstock as infamous beyond expression. I have very little respect for those men who endeavor to put down vice by lying; and very little respect for a society that would keep in its employ such a leprous agent."

It is greatly to be regretted that in the last quarter of the nineteenth century such a base specimen of humanity as Anthony Comstock has been selected to be the protector of public morals, to be a champion of the Church, and a censor of the mails, of medical and physiological literature, and of Radical and Freethought publications. If free America is to have a censor of the press and of her mails, it would certainly be desired that a man might be selected to discharge the duties of the office who possessed some qualifications for the position, and who exhibited, at least, an average amount of morality, decency, honesty, and truthfulness. Can members of the Christian society which for years has employed this man and made him their active agent and representative, expect to add to their own credit or to that of the Christian religion by employing and sustaining such a despicable character as Anthony Comstock—the Matthew Hopkins of the nineteenth century?

RECAPITULATION.

FOR the convenience of the reader a brief summary of the most conspicuous acts of the characters treated in the foregoing pages will here be given. As the first few characters are regarded, more or less, as myths, therefore there is not any very marked conduct to be mentioned in connection with them. First:

Jesus. His miracles. His deity. His moral teachings. He did not respect the rights of property. As a communist. He taught submission to wrong. His professions to pardon sin. He exhibited an imperfect sense of justice.

Jesus and Jesuism. The progress of Jesuism.

Peter and the great compromise.

The Four Evangelists. Evidence that all the gospels had one origin. The writers do not claim to be eye-witnesses. What was the character of the early Christians? Christianity always intolerant. Christian admissions against the Scriptures.

Paulism versus Jesuism. The early Christian Church.

Paul was disagreeably self-conceited and boastful. In his great desire to get followers, he became a hypocrite, was all things too all men; and he justified dissembling and lying if they contributed to the glory of God. His notions concerning women have caused much of the oppressive tyranny under which the female sex in all Christian countries have suffered during the last eighteen centuries.

Clement of Rome, Ignatius, Justin Martyr, Polycarp, Papias, Irenæus, Tertullian, and Origen, early Fathers of the Church, are chiefly famous for the writings attributed to them. The Catholic Church is founded more upon their writings than upon the Bible; but modern research is fast proving that their writings are nothing more than a record of the legends and traditions floating about during the early years of the Christian Church, mixed with a due proportion of pagan "mysteries," changed to suit the purposes of the new religion.

St. Victor was one of the first bishops of Rome, and began the movement which ultimately placed the bishops of Rome at the head of the Christian Church.

St. Anthony is famous chiefly on account of his laziness and filthiness, wearing nothing but a sheepskin, which he never changed, and never washed his body.

St. Paul the Hermit was the founder of the Christian system of monkery. He was a fanatic who lived more like a beast than a human being.

Stephen I., bishop of Rome, was notorious for his quarrelsome disposition, being constantly embroiled in bitter contentions with his brother bishops.

Constantine placed Christianity upon the throne. An execrable parricide, he put to death the two Licinii, the husband and son of his sister. He did not even spare his own children; and the Empress Fausta, the wife of this monster, was strangled in her bath by his orders. Upon consulting the pagan priests of the empire as to what expiation he should make for his crime, he was repulsed with horror by the priests, who exclaimed, "Far from hence be parricides, whom the gods never pardon." After this a Christian promised him pardon for his crimes if he should become purified in the waters of baptism, so the emperor became a Christian.

Eusebius, the father, or rather the manufacturer of ecclesiastical history, was superstitious, crafty, a time-server, a partisan, and a flatterer.

The works of Eusebius are a remarkable instance of the prostitution of great talents in the cause of mental degradation and slavery.

Callistus was a notorious thief and defaulter, who by a strange combination of circumstances was elevated from the workhouse to the Roman see.

Theodosius caused the massacre in cold blood of fifteen thousand innocent people. His persecution of the Arians has made his name forever infamous—outside of the Christian Church.

St. Cyril caused the murder of the talented and beautiful young philosopher, Hypatia, and through his machinations the famous Alexandrian library was destroyed.

Siricus derives his principal importance from his propagation of priestly celibacy in the fourth century.

Dioscorus, bishop of Alexandria, assisted by a friend, assaulted and beat Flavianus, bishop of Constantinople, so severely that he died in three days; and this in the presence of his brother bishops, at the celebrated " Robber Council " of Ephesus.

St. Augustine, in his writings, laid down the laws and precepts by which the Church has been enabled to enslave, debase, and degrade mankind, and to make it resemble the ideal of total depravity upon which they build their scheme of salvation.

Simeon Stylites, the great ascetic, fanatic, and saint, was noted for his laziness, piety, and filthy habits. He lived on the top of a pillar until it resembled an exaggerated and unclean parrot's perch, and finally starved and stifled in the odor and effluvia of sanctity and filth—too lazy to descend from his pillar for food or fresh air.

Clovis the Great deliberately assassinated all the princes belonging to his family, but he spared no pains to propitiate the bishop of Rome, who, in consideration of his piety and usefulness, conferred upon him the title of " The Most Christian King, and Eldest Son of the Church."

Sixtus, the third bishop of Rome of that name, was guilty of incest and rape. When accused of the crime, he caused the accuser to be poisoned.

Virgilius was distinguished for his perfidy, debauchery, and crime. His life is one long record of abomination. He was a suborner and a sodomite, a knave, a miser, and an assassin. He killed with a club a poor child who resisted his infamous embraces. Notwithstanding his crimes, he is now worshiped as a saint by all good Catholics.

Gregory the Great destroyed the monuments of Roman magnificence, set fire to the Palatine Library, destroyed the works of Titus Livy and the most famous Latin poets because they opposed superstitious worship, and he made war upon everything which bore the name of art or science.

Boniface III. was elevated to the see of Rome by Phocas, one of the most bloodthirsty monsters that ever cursed the earth.

Irene, empress of the East, one of the most zealous and pious of Christians, put out the eyes of her own son.

Pepin, King of France, was allied in succession with two of the popes of Rome in their iniquitous projects; and in order to make reparation to the Church for his usurpation of the crown of France, and the murder of his brother, he surrendered to the holy see the domains of Romagna which he had taken from the Lombards.

Charlemagne invaded Lombardy, deprived his nephews of their inheritance, despoiled his brother-in-law to punish him for having undertaken their defense, carried him to Lyons in chains, and condemned him to end his days in prison. Then Leo III. placed a crown of gold upon his head, and made him one of the chief pillars of the Christian Church.

Paschal I. put out the eyes and cut off the heads of Theodorus and Leo, two high officers of the Church, because they criticised his iniquities. After his death the people wished to drag his body through the streets of Rome, so great was their detestation of his crimes.

Popess Joan mounted the chair of St. Peter, celebrated mass, and created bishops. She became enciente by a cardinal and died in the pangs of child-birth, in the midst of a religious ceremony.

Nicholas I., for a large sum of money, not only pardoned but virtually endorsed the ravishment of Judith, daughter of Charles the Bold, by the count of Flanders. He was always ready to anathematize or flatter for gold. A French bishop, in a letter to this pope, used the following language: "Thy cohort of priests, soiled with adulteries, incests, rapes, and assassinations, is well worthy to form thy infamous court, for Rome is the residence of demons, and thou, pope, art its Satan."

While Sergius was pope, he led publicly a life soiled with debaucheries with the famous courtesan Marozia, a monster of depravity who committed incests with her sons and grand-sons.

John XI., son of Marozia, lived in incest with his mother while occupying the papal chair, as did also his brother, John XII. These two popes surpassed their infamous mother in vileness. They were guilty of profanity, blasphemy, adultery, incest with their mother, and murder.

John XIII. cut off the nose and lips of the Prefect Peter, and originated the ceremony of baptizing church bells.

Boniface VII. was the son of a Roman prostitute._ His life was one long succession of infamies. Murders, poisonings, and judicial assassinations succeeded each other in such quick succession during his reign that writers of that time called him "Maliface."

Benedict IX. was made pope at the age of twelve years, and immediately surrendered himself to excessive depravity and the most shameful debaucheries. Twice he was driven in disgrace from the papal chair, and twice he returned. During his pontificate there was a double schism in the Church, so that there were three popes reigning at the same time.

Hildebrand, the poisoner of popes, the most deceitful of priests, usurped the pontifical seat under the name of Gregory VII. He excited civil wars and filled Germany and Italy with disorder, carnage, and murder. He excommunicated the emperor of Germany, took from him his title of king, freed his people from the oath of obedience, excited other princes against him, and at last reduced him to such a state of misfortune that he became almost insane.

Adrian IV., the son of an English friar, compelled the Emperor Barbarossa to act as his groom. The brave and noble **Arnold** of Brescia was burned to death by this vice-gerent of the Most High.

St. Dominic was sent forth by Innocent III. to persecute with fire and sword and unheard-of torments the unfortunate Waldenses. He swept through the land like a pestilence, the cross in one hand and the torch in the other, and sixty thousand victims were buried in the ruins of one city alone, merely because they could not subscribe to the dogmas of the Church. For more than twenty years Innocent III. carried on the persecutions of the Albigenses. His able and efficient agent in this horrible work, Simon de Montfort, was a monster of villainy and cruelty. His bloodthirsty nature made him a willing assistant of the Church in its relentless persecutions of the unfortunate unbelievers.

Innocent IV. betrayed the Emperor Frederic, and excited civil war in his dominions. Under his reign, the mendicant monks became the plague of Europe. He died of a disease brought on by his debaucheries.

Peter the Hermit inaugurated a series of crusades which cost Europe millions of lives and wasted untold treasures. He was a fanatic of the most dangerous kind, but is now among the saints of the Romish Church

Boniface VIII. became pope after having assassinated his predecessor. He outraged the people, defied kings, pursued with hatred the Ghibelines, the partisans of the emperor of Germany, and invented the jubilees, which drew so much of the earnings of the poor into the coffers of the Church. The archbishop of Narbonne accused him of being a simoniac, an assassin, and a usurer, of living in concubinage with his two nieces, and of having children by them, and of having employed the riches extorted from the poor to bribe the Saracens to invade Italy.

John XXII. seized the tiara, seated himself on the pontifical throne, and proclaimed himself pope. In order to strengthen his usurpation, he launched his anathemas against the emperor of Germany and the king of France, persecuted sectarians, burned heretics, freed people from their allegiance, armed princes for war against each other, invaded kingdoms, preached new crusades, sold benefices, and extorted from the faithful upwards of twenty-five millions of florins.

Clement VI. bought from the celebrated Joanna of Naples the country of Avignon, promising therefor three hundred thousand florins of gold, which he never paid, and declared her innocent of the murder of Andreas, her husband, whom she had caused to be assassinated.

Innocent VI. was elected pope after subscribing to a constitution and regulations framed by the cardinals for the protection of their interests. Immediately upon assuming the pontifical dignity he annulled his agreement and violated his oath by virtue of his infallibility. One of his minions assassinated the celebrated Rienzi. The reign of this pope was characterized by the persecutions of the Fratricellists.

Under Urban VI. commenced the great schism which divided the Church for so many years. After plotting the assassination of Queen Joanna of Naples, he was driven from Rome. After a short absence, he returned to the holy city and died of poison. During his pontificate the morals of the clergy had become terribly corrupted.

The sketch of the antipopes and counter-popes gives a charming picture of the " one true Church " during a period when it was presided over by a plurality of popes, each claiming to be the only true and infallible representative of Deity on earth. For years they convulsed Europe with their wars, during which they caused the deaths of untold thousands of innocent men.

Of St. Ursula very little is known. Her name, however, is one of the brightest in the long list of Catholic saints. As a general thing, the less historical facts there are known concerning Christian saints, the better their reputation for morality stands the test of modern criticism.

John XXIII., a most infamous monster, usurped the pontifical throne and terrified the cardinals into confirming him in his position. A terrible and bloody war between three rival popes, in which all southern Europe was involved,

followed this act. A general council assembled and proceeded to depose John. The bishops and cardinals accused
him of murders, incests, poisoning, and sodomy; of having
seduced and carried on a sacrilegious intercourse with three
hundred religious women; of having violated three sisters;
and of having imprisoned a whole family in order that he
might act out his pleasure with the different members of it.
He was eventually deposed.

Martin V., a vile and despicable pope, covered entire
provinces with woful disaster, and caused the massacre of
multitudes. His terrible decree against the Hussites spread
devastation all over Germany. He caused the bones of
Wickliffe to be burnt, and was guilty of private assassination
and the slaughter of thousands and thousands of innocent
men, women, and children.

Paul II. was a vile, vain, cruel, and licentious pontiff, whose
chief delight consisted in torturing heretics with heated bra-
ziers and infernal instruments of torment. He died a victim
of his gluttonous intemperance.

Torquemada, the human hyena, instituted the infernal
Inquisition in Spain, and, during the eighteen years he
was inquisitor-general, burnt 12,000 persons alive and 7,000
in effigy, imprisoned 90,000 for life, and tortured with all the
hellish cruelty that ingenuity can devise over 100,000 more.

Ferdinand and Isabella. The sketch of these sovereigns
embraces an account of their efforts to extirpate heresy in
their dominions. The hapless Moors and Jews were driven
out of Spain, and the diabolical fires of the Inquisition were
lit throughout the kingdom. As the champions of Catholic
Christianity these two otherwise humane rulers appear in the
character of cruel and relentless bigots.

Alexander VI., was the most hideous monster whose name
blackens the annals of Rome. All historians admit that this
pope was one of the most dreadful of all men who have
affrighted the world. His career was one prolonged carnival
of the most monstrous crimes that the mind of man can conceive. Delivering himself up to incest and sodomy, debauch-

ery, assassination, and murder, and reveling in orgies, the mere description of which suffices to sicken the reader, he finally himself partook of the poison he had destined for two cardinals and ended his execrable life.

Martin Luther was a man of ungovernable passions and insane violence, who, becoming involved in a quarrel with the pope, was excommunicated; and then, in mad opposition, he threw off the obligations of his monkish vows, and with a band of protesting adherents undertook to play the part of a petty pope himself in Germany. He spent his life in fighting the mother Church and quarreling with his Protestant companions. He manifested the intensest hatred toward, and violently attacked everything not agreeable to his own will. He advocated persecution, denounced the discoveries of science, inveighed against Copernicus, calling him "an old fool," passed a stormy life in fighting religious foes and wrangling with his followers, and died, according to Mr. Segur, "forlorn of God, blaspheming to the very end."

John Calvin, a cold, calculating, cruel bigot, heartless and hypocritical, went to Geneva, and upon the ruins of the republic established the most terrible theocracy ever known among men. He sought to fasten the iron yoke of his detestable doctrines upon the necks of the people, and pounced upon all who opposed him with sanguinary ferocity. His two most diabolical acts were the execution of James Gruet, the poet, and the roasting to death of Michael Servetus in a slow fire of green oak. The details of his acts of cold-blooded cruelty excite the horror even of a Christian.

Loyola and the Jesuits. Giving a graphic account of the career of the fanatical founder of the Society of Jesus, and of the rise, spread, workings, and plottings of his dark and dangerous order. Historical facts are adduced to show that it has been the secret source of all the horrors and enormities, tortures and crimes, that papal Rome has inflicted on mankind since its institution in 1538. This long indictment includes every conceivable atrocity of secret assassination and wholesale massacre.

Henry VIII. divorced two of his six wives, cut off the heads of two others, lit the fires of persecution, in which Catholics were burnt for recognizing the pope, and Protestants were burnt for not recognizing himself as head of the the Church of England. Charles Dickins says he was a "disgrace to human nature, and a blot of blood and grease upon the history of England."

Hernando Cortez. A brave but bigoted Spanish adventurer, who, under pretense of propagating the Christian religion in the New World, practiced the most inhuman barbarity upon the natives. Wholesale butchery marked his march through Mexico. Four millions of the population perished. Cortez found this newly discovered empire a heathen paradise, and left it a Christian waste.

Francisco Pizarro discovered and conquered Peru, and attempted to Christianize it by some of the most infamous acts of butchery and treachery that stain the records of crime. He massacred or burnt at the stake all who offered him the least opposition. He killed and ravaged and robbed in the name of the Church, and proved himself the most perfidious of those monsters of religion and cruelty who made it their life-work to reduce the aborigines of America to slavery.

Charles V., the most powerful monarch of the sixteenth century, introduced the Inquisition into his German provinces, erected scaffolds that were never empty, and lighted fires that never lacked for human fuel. In pursuance of his bloody edicts one hundred thousand Netherlanders were burned, beheaded, or buried alive.

Philip II., the crowned cut-throat, called the "Demon of the South," spent his whole life in the extirpation of heresy. He plotted the butchery of St. Bartholomew seventeen years before the hellish deed was done. He converted his dominions into a vast cemetery for the bodies of hundreds of thousands of his subjects executed upon the scaffold or burnt at the stake. He poisoned his own son, Don Carlos. The devilish details of his reign exhibit a cruelty and treachery with which nothing else in history will compare.

The Duke of Alva, one of the most ferocious and blood-thirsty monsters to which the Catholic Church has given birth, was a man of prodigious vices and no virtues. His career in the Netherlands was one saturnalia of blood and butchery. His horrible deeds of cruelty, detailed in this sketch, are sufficient to cause the heart of humanity to shudder for all time, and cause Nero and Caligula to be considered humane in comparison with him. Suffice it to say, he nearly depopulated the Dutch Provinces and converted them into a slaughter pen.

John Knox, a fiery, relentless, hard-hearted Scotch bigot, violated his vows to the Catholic faith by marriage, participated in the assassination of Cardinal Beatoun, cowardly fled to England and Geneva whenever he felt himself insecure at home; and whenever, with safety to himself, he could incite his countrymen to insurrection, he marched through Scotland at the head of a band of ranting preachers with the Gospel in one hand and a fire-brand in the other, burning churches and monasteries, and destroying the choicest libraries and works of art; conspired against his queen, the beautiful and unfortunate Mary, being accessory to the brutal assassination of her private secretary, instigated many dark deeds of blood and treachery, forged a letter, and by his foul plotting and heartless persecution became the most guilty accomplice in the base and barbarous execution of Mary, Queen of Scots.

Thomas Munzer was a German fanatic who, with a troop of violent Anabaptists, went through Germany burning and plundering, and spreading devastation and death. He and his band of outlaws caused the death of forty thousand people.

Mary of England was better known as "Bloody Mary." Her reign is one long catalogue of horrors. She caused to be burnt at the stake Cranmer, Ridley, Latimer, together with three hundred men, women, and children.

Catherine de Medici led a life of poisoning and crime, procured the massacre of St. Bartholomew, in which one hundred thousand Huguenots were brutally butchered, and poisoned her own son. Her execrable career makes a great blood-blot on the history of France.

The reign of Queen Elizabeth was one of turmoil and bloodshed. She established the High Commission, a terrible tribunal for the punishment of heresy against the Protestant faith, filled all the jails in her kingdom with prisoners, invented new and more cruel instruments of torture, murdered Mary of Scotland after keeping her in prison nineteen years, and put to death two hundred and four of her Catholic subjects on account of their religion.

Julius III. was a depraved debauchee and sodomite.

Pius IV. was notorious for his avarice, licentiousness, and gluttony. He filled the papal palace with courtesans and beautiful boys for the purpose of satisfying his sensual passions and assuaging his lubricity.

Pius V. was a heartless and sanguinary wretch whose chief delight seemed to consist in personally presiding over the tortures of heretics.

Gregory XIII. was accessory to the bloody butchery of St. Bartholomew. After the massacre he caused the cannon in the castle of San Angelo to be fired, published a jubilee throughout Europe, and caused a medal to be struck to commemorate the slaughter of one hundred thousand men, women, and children.

Sixtus V. announced that, like Christ, he had come to bring a sword, not peace. He celebrated his coronation by hanging sixty heretics. He was a cold and crafty man, and as vile a villain as ever sat in the chair of St. Peter.

James I. murdered Sir Walter Raleigh, filled England and Scotland with religious rancor and persecution, and caused the Bible to be translated.

Paul V. incited insurrection among the English Catholics, encouraged the terrible Gunpowder Plot, caused the body of the celebrated author, Dominis, to be burned with his books in the public square, and, according to the historian, wallowed like a hog in the most stinking and disgusting odors of adultery and sodomy that can be imagined.

The article on the Persecutions of Witches gives a summary account of witchcraft in different countries and ages, of the cruel codes, persecutions, and punishments imposed against it throughout Christendom, together with details of some of the most noteworthy trials.

That on Protestant Persecutions gives a succinct history of the cruelty and tyranny perpetrated by the Protestant portion of the Christian Church from the Reformation to the present day. The details of the horrible and diabolical tortures inflicted by Protestant inquisitors constitute a bloody chapter indeed. Adherence to the Catholic faith was punished as the most atrocious of crimes. Massacre and murder kept pace with the progress of the doctrines of Luther and Calvin in the Old World and the New. The particulars of the inhuman barbarities practiced by Protestant persecutors are sufficient to sicken the most callous-hearted reader. Like the Catholics, they sought to extirpate heresy by fire and sword.

Urban VIII. secured a seat in the papal chair by treachery and force of arms; poisoned his opponents in the sacred college, and made Rome the theatre of violence, pillage, murder, and the most terrible atrocities; pursued a policy of intrigue which involved France and all Europe in a long and bloody war; assassinated the young duke of Urbino; handed Galileo over to the terrible tortures of the Inquisition, and died cursing and blaspheming.

James II. made war upon his Protestant subjects, turning loose upon them a ruthless band of outlaws under the cruel Kirk, who robbed and murdered them without mercy; commissioned the monstrous Jeffreys to go through the country holding his "Bloody Assize," and burn and hang indiscriminately; sent the ferocious Claverhouse to carry death and ruin among the covenanters of Scotland. His reign was a time of misery and terror.

Louis XIV. repealed the edict of Nantes, and attempted the total destruction of the Huguenots. He put to death or drove into exile the industrial population of France, made Paris a vast almshouse, and reduced the poor peasantry to starvation. His reign was a period of disaster and national decay.

Innocent X. was a cruel, licentious pope who destroyed the city of Castro, placed the power of the papacy in the hands of a prostitute, taught the violation of oaths, and abandoned himself to the most disgusting debauchery.

St. Liguori was a great light of the Catholic Church, and promulgated the most execrable axioms ever taught, the gist of which was that deception, perjury, and crime were not only justifiable, but even praiseworthy when perpetrated for the interest of the Church and the greater glory of God.

Pius VI. was guilty of sodomy, adultery, incest, and murder; organized bands of brigands who ravaged the papal States; committed the most atrocious acts, poisoning and massacring all the French they could find; incited bands of fanatics to burn harvests, poison rivers and fountains, and plunge their hands in the blood of his foes.

The article on Christianity and Slavery portrays Christian opposition to freedom and its affiliation with the worst form of human slavery the world has known.

That devoted to Sinful Clergymen portrays near three hundred instances of gross licentiousness, bigamy, adultery, fornication, sodomy, and numerous other crimes.

Anthony Comstock has proved himself equal to almost any of his Christian predecessors in the work of arresting, persecuting, prosecuting, and ruining his fellow-beings. In the shameful qualities of falsehood, intrigue, entrapping, decoying unsuspecting victims, inveigling and tempting his fellow-beings to commit offenses, that he might be able to punish them, he stands without a peer in the Christian ranks. He boasts of having driven fifteen persons to suicide, and it is believed that he has driven an equal number to an involuntary death. The charge of perjury, too, hangs over him to that extent that he will find it impossible to remove it. As a champion of morality and decency, he is perhaps one of the most sensual, vile, and corrupt that has lived since the Christian rule began.

CONCLUDING REMARKS.

THERE is but one conclusion at which the readers of these pages can arrive, and that is that the religion of Christianity has been one of cruel intolerance and bloody persecution. From the time it came to be a political power, early in the fourth century, until the present time, it has shown the same illiberal, intolerant, and exacting spirit. It has been unwilling, when it has had the power to prevent it, that any other creed should live by the side of it; it has been ready to hunt down, torture, rack, impale, hang, and burn every independent man and woman who has presumed to dissent from its prescribed line of belief. As Ingersoll forcibly states the facts: "In the name of God every possible crime has been committed— every conceivable outrage has been perpetrated. Brave men, tender and loving women, beautiful girls, and prattling babes have been exerminated in the name of Jesus Christ. For more than fifty generations the Church has carried the black flag. Her vengeance has been measured only by her power. During all these years of infamy no heretic has been forgiven. With the heart of a fiend she has hated; with the clutch of avarice she has grasped; with the jaws of a dragon she has devoured; pitiless as famine, merciless as fire, with the conscience of a serpent. Such is the history of the Church of God."

The work of persecution, torture, tyranny, and death to those who dared to dissent, as a matter of course, existed longer in the Romish Church than in its offspring, the Protestant, but this was only because its opportunities were more favorable to it. So far as the newer Church has had the power and the opportunity, it has shown the same bloodthirsty, ferocious, tyrannizing, and persecuting despotism. The world has advanced not a little in the last three centuries, and this progress has exercised a very modifying influence upon the newer form of faith. If Protestantism has been less bloody than Romanism, it is not because it is inherently better, but because its power for evil has been materially lessened. Under the same circumstances and with the same power, one would be no better than the other. With unlimited control, either would arrest, torture, burn, behead, and hang to-day with as much zest and pleasure as ever it did before.

Ingersoll says : " Men and women have been burned for thinking there was but one God; that there was none; that the Holy Ghost is younger than God; that God was somewhat older than his son; for insisting that good works will save a man without faith; that faith will not do without good works; for declaring that a sweet babe will not be burned eternally because its parents failed to have its head wet by a priest; for speaking of God as though he had a nose; for denying that Christ was his own father; for contending that three persons, rightly added together, make more than one; for believing in purgatory; for denying the reality of hell; for pretending that priests can forgive sins; for preaching that God is an essence; for denying that witches rode through the air on sticks; for doubting the total depravity of the human heart; for laughing at irresistible grace, predestination, and particular redemption; for denying that good bread could be made of the body of a dead man; for pretending that the pope was not managing this world for God, and in place of God; for disputing the efficacy of a vicarious atonement; for thinking that the Virgin Mary was born like other people; for thinking that a man's rib was hardly sufficient to make a good-sized woman; for denying that God used his finger for a pen; for asserting that prayers are not answered; that diseases are not sent to punish unbelief; for denying the authority of the Bible; for having a Bible in their possession; for attending mass, and for refusing to attend; for wearing a surplice; for carrying a cross, and for refusing; for being a

Catholic, and for being a Protestant; for being an Episcopalian, a Presbyterian, a Baptist, and for being a Quaker. In short, every virtue has been a crime, and every crime a virtue. The Church has burned honesty and rewarded hypocrisy, and all this she did because it was commanded by a book—a book that man had been taught implicitly to believe long before they knew one word that was in it. They had been taught that to doubt the truth of this book—to examine it, even—was a crime of such enormity that it could not be forgiven, either in this world or in the next.

"Protestants and Catholics vied with each other in the work of enslaving the human mind. For ages they were rivals in the infamous effort to rid the earth of honest people. They infested every country, every city, town, hamlet, and family. They appealed to the worst passions of the human heart. They sowed the seeds of discord and hatred in every land. Brother denounced brother, wives informed against their husbands, mothers accused their children, dungeons were crowded with the innocent; the flesh of the good and the true rotted in the clasp of chains; the flames devoured the heroic, and, in the name of the most merciful God, his children were exterminated with famine, sword, and fire. Over the wild waves of battle rose and fell the banner of Jesus Christ. For sixteen hundred years the robes of the Church were red with innocent blood. The ingenuity of Christians was exhausted in devising punishment severe enough to be inflicted upon other Christians who honestly and sincerely differed with them upon any point whatever.

"Give any orthodox Church the power, and to-day they would punish heresy with the whip, and chain, and fire. As long as a Church deems a certain belief essential to salvation, just so long it will kill and burn if it has the power. Why should the Church pity a man whom her God hates? Why should she show mercy to a kind and noble heretic whom her God will burn in eternal fire? Why should a Christian be better than his God? It is impossible for the imagination to conceive of a greater atrocity than has been perpetrated by the Church.

" Let it be remembered that all Churches have persecuted heretics to the extent of their power. Every nerve in the human body capable of pain has been sought out and touched by the Church. Toleration has increased only when and where the power of the Church has diminished. From Augustine until now the spirit of the Christian has remained the same. There has been the same intolerance, the same undying hatred of all who think for themselves, the same determination to crush out of the human brain all knowledge inconsistent with the ignorant creed.

" Every Church pretends that it has a revelation from God, and that this revelation must be given to the people through the Church; that the Church acts through its priests, and that ordinary mortals must be content with a revelation, not from God, but from the Church. Had the people submitted to this preposterous claim, of course there could have been but one Church, and that Church never could have advanced. It might have retrograded, because it is not necessary to think or investigate in order to forget. Without heresy there could have been no progress.

" The highest type of the orthodox Christian does not forget. Neither does he learn. He neither advances nor recedes. He is a living fossil, imbedded in that rock called faith. He makes no effort to better his condition, because all his strength is exhausted in keeping other people from improving theirs. The supreme desire of his heart is to force all others to adopt his creed, and in order to accomplish this object he denounces all kinds of Freethinking as a crime, and this crime he calls heresy. When he had the power, heresy was the most terrible and formidable of words. It meant confiscation, exile, imprisonment, torture, and death.

" In those days the cross and rack were inseperable companions. Across the open Bible lay the sword and fagot. Not content with burning such heretics as were alive, they even tried the dead, in order that the Church might rob their

wives and children. The property of all heretics was confiscated, and on this account they charged the dead with being
heretical—indicted, as it were, their dust, to the end that the
Church might clutch the bread of orphans. Learned divines
discussed the propriety of tearing out the tongues of heretics
before they were burned, and the general opinion was that
this ought to be done, so that the heretics should not be able,
by uttering blasphemies, to shock the Christians who were
burning them. With a mixture of ferocity and Christianity,
the priests insisted that heretics ought to be burned at a slow
fire, giving as a reason, that more time was given them for
repentance.

"No wonder that Jesus Christ said, 'I come not to bring
peace but a sword!' Every priest regarded himself as the
agent of God. He answered all questions by authority, and
to treat him with disrespect was an insult offered to God.
No one was asked to think, but all were commanded to
obey.

"In 1208 the Inquisition was established. Seven years
afterward, the fourth council of the Lateran enjoined all kings
and rulers to swear an oath that they would exterminate
heretics from their dominions. The sword of the Church
was unsheathed, and the world was at the mercy of ignorant
and infuriated priests, whose eyes feasted upon the agonies
they inflicted. Acting as they believed, or pretended to
believe, under the command of God, stimulated by the hope
of infinite reward in another world, hating heretics with
every drop of their bestial blood, savage beyond description,
merciless beyond conception, these infamous priests, in a
kind of frenzied joy, leaped upon the helpless victims of their
rage. They crushed their bones in iron boots, tore their
quivering flesh with iron hooks and pincers, cut off their lips
and eyelids, pulled out their nails, and into the bleeding
quick thrust needles, tore out their tongues, extinguished their
eyes, stretched them upon racks, flayed them alive, crucified
them with the head downward, exposed them to wild beasts,
burned them at the stake, mocked their cries and groans,

ravished their wives, robbed their children, and then prayed God to finish the holy work in hell.

"Millions upon millions were sacrified upon the altars of bigotry. The Catholic burned the Lutheran, the Lutheran burned the Catholic; the Episcopalian tortured the Presbyterian, the Presbyterian tortured the Episcopalian. Every denomination killed all it could of every other; and each Christian felt in duty bound to exterminate every other Christian who denied the smallest fraction of his creed. According to the creed. of every Church, slavery leads to heaven, liberty leads to hell. It was claimed that God had founded the Church, and that to deny the authority of the Church was to be a traitor to God, and consequently an ally of the devil. To torture and destroy one of the soldiers of Satan was a duty no good Christian cared to neglect. Nothing can be sweeter than to earn the gratitude of God by killing your own enemies. Such a mingling of profit and revenge, of heaven for yourself and damnation for those you dislike, is a temptation that your ordinary Christian never resists.

"According to the theologians, God, the Father of us all, wrote a letter to his children. The children have always differed somewhat as to the meaning of this letter. In consequence of these honest differences, those brothers began to cut out each other's hearts. In every land, where this letter from God has been read, the children to whom and for whom it was written have been filled with hatred and malice. They have imprisoned and murdered each other, and the wives and children of each other."

Again the same writer says: "For thousands of years a thinker was hunted down like an escaped convict. To him who had braved the Church every door was shut, every knife was open. To shelter him from the wild storm, to give him a crust of bread when dying, to put a cup of water to his cracked and bleeding lips; these were all crimes not one of which the Church ever did forgive; and with the justice taught of her God, his helpless children were exterminated as scorpions and vipers.

"Who at the present day can imagine the courage, the devotion to principle, the intellectual and moral grandeur it once required to be an Infidel, to brave the Church, her racks, her fagots, her dungeons, her tongues of fire; to defy and scorn her heaven and her hell, her devil and her God? They were the noblest sons of earth. They were the real saviors of our race, the destroyers of superstition and the creators of science. They were the real Titans who bared their grand foreheads to all the thunderbolts of all the gods.

"The Church has been, and still is, the great robber. She has rifled not only the pockets but the brains of the world. She is the stone at the sepulchre of liberty; the upas tree in whose shade the intellect of man has withered; the Gorgon beneath whose gaze the human heart has turned to stone.

"Christianity has always opposed every forward movement of the human race. Across the highway of progress it has always been building breastworks of Bibles, tracts, commentaries, prayer-books, creeds, dogmas, and platforms; and at every advance the Christians have gathered behind these heaps of rubbish and shot the poisoned arrows of malice at the soldiers of freedom.

"And even the Liberal Christian of to-day has his holy of holies, and in the niche of the temple of his heart has his idol. He still clings to a part of the old superstition, and all the pleasant memories of the old belief linger in the horizon of his thoughts like a sunset. We associate the memory of those we love with the religion of our childhood. It seems almost a sacrilege to rudely destroy the idols that our fathers worshiped, and turn their sacred and beautiful truths into the silly fables of barbarism. Some throw away the Old Testament and cling to the New, while others give up everything except the idea that there is a personal God, and that in some wonderful way we are the objects of his care."

On another occasion he said: "Through all the centuries gone, the mind of man has been beleaguered by the mailed hosts of superstition. Slowly and painfully has advanced the army of deliverance. Hated by those they wished to rescue, despised by those they were dying to save, these grand soldiers, these immortal deliverers, have fought without thanks, labored without applause, suffered without pity, and they have died execrated and abhorred. For the good of mankind they accepted isolation, poverty, and calumny. They gave up all, sacrificed all, lost all but truth and respect.

"No effort has been, in any age of the world, spared to crush out opposition. The Church used painting, music, and architecture simply to degrade mankind. But there are men that nothing can awe. There have been at all times brave spirits that dared even the gods. Some proud head has always been above the waves. In every age some Diogenes has sacrificed to all the gods. True genius never cowers, and there is always some Samson feeling for the pillars of authority.

"Cathedrals and domes, and chimes and chants, temples frescoed and groined and carved, and gilded with gold, altars and tapers, and paintings of virgin and babe, censer and chalice, chasuble, paten, and alb; organs and anthems, and incense rising to the winged and blest, maniple, amice, and stole, crosses and crosiers, tiaras and crowns, mitres and missals and masses, rosaries, relics and robes, martyrs and saints, and windows stained as with the blood of Christ, never for one moment awed the brave, proud spirit of a true Infidel. He knew that all the pomp and glitter had been purchased with liberty—that priceless jewel of the soul. In looking at the cathedral he remembered the dungeon. The music of the organ was not loud enough to drown the clank of fetters. He could not forget that the taper had lighted the fagot. He knew that the cross adorned the hilt of the sword, and so, where others worshiped, he wept and scorned.

"The doubter, the investigator, the Infidel, have been the saviors of liberty. This truth is beginning to be realized, and the intellectual are beginning to honor the brave thinkers of the past.

"But the Church is as unforgiving as ever, and still wonders why any Infidel should be wicked enough to endeavor to destroy her power.

"I will tell the Church why.

"You have imprisoned the human mind; you have been the enemy of liberty; you have burned us at the stake, wasted us upon slow fires, torn our flesh with iron; you have covered us with chains, treated us as outcasts; you have filled the world with fear; you have taken our wives and children from our arms; you have confiscated our property; you have denied us the right to testify in courts of justice; you have branded us with infamy; you have torn out our tongues; you have refused us burial. In the name of your religion, you have robbed us of every right; and after having inflicted upon us every evil that can be inflicted in this world, you have fallen upon your knees, and with clasped hands, implored your God to torment us forever.

"Can you wonder that we hate your doctrines, that we despise your creeds, that we feel proud to know that we are beyond your power, that we are free in spite of you, that we can express our honest thought, and that the whole world is grandly rising into the blessed light?

"Can you wonder that we point with pride to the fact that Infidelity has ever been found battling for the rights of man, for the liberty of conscience, and for the happiness of all?

"Can you wonder that we are proud to know that we have always been disciples of Reason and soldiers of Freedom; that we have denounced tyranny and superstition, and have kept our hands unstained with human blood?

"We deny that religion is the end or object of this life. When it is so considered it becomes destructive of happiness —the real end of life. It becomes a hydra-headed monster, reaching in terrible coils from the heavens, and thrusting its thousand fangs into the bleeding, quivering hearts of men. It devours their substance, builds palaces for God (who dwells not in temples made with hands), and allows his children to die in huts and hovels. It fills the earth with mourning, heaven with hatred, the present with fear, and all the future with despair.

" Virtue is a subordination of the passions to the intellect. It is to act in accordance with your highest convictions. It does not consist in believing, but in doing.

"This is the sublime truth that the Infidels in all ages have uttered. They have handed the torch from one to the other through all the years that have fled. Upon the altar of Reason they have kept the sacred fire, and through the long midnight of faith, they feed the divine flame.

" Infidelity is liberty; all religion is slavery. In every creed, man is the slave of God, woman is the slave of man, and the sweet children are the slaves of all.

" We do not want creeds; we want knowledge, we want happiness.

" And yet we are told by the Church that we have accomplished nothing; that we are simply destroyers; that we tear down without building again.

" Is it nothing to free the mind? Is it nothing to civilize mankind? Is it nothing to fill the world with light, with discovery, with science? Is it nothing to dignify man and exalt the intellect? Is it nothing to grope your way into the dreary prisons, the damp and dropping dungeons, the dark and silent cells, where the souls of men are chained to the floors of stone; to greet them like a ray of light, like the song of a bird, the murmur of a stream; to see the dull eyes open and grow slowly bright; to feel yourself grasped by the shrunken and unused hands, and hear yourself thanked by a strange and hollow voice?

" Is it nothing to conduct these souls gradually into the blessed light of day, to let them see again the happy fields, the sweet, green earth, and hear the everlasting music of the waves? Is it nothing to make men wipe the dust from their swollen knees, the tears from their blanched and furrowed cheeks? Is it a small thing to reave the heavens of an insatiate monster and write upon the eternal dome, glittering with stars, the grand word—FREEDOM?

" Is it a small thing to quench the flames of hell with the holy tears of pity, to unbind the martyr from the stake, break all the chains, put out the fires of civil war, stay the sword of the fanatic, and tear the bloody hands of the Church from the white throat of Science?

"Is it a small thing to make men truly free, to destroy the dogmas of ignorance, prejudice, and power, the poisoned fables of superstition, and drive from the beautiful face of the earth the fiend of Fear?

"It does seem as though the most zealous Christian must at times entertain some doubt as to the divine origin of his religion. For eighteen hundred years the doctrine has been preached. For more than a thousand years the Church had, to a great extent, control of the civilized world, and what has been the result? Are the Christian nations patterns of charity and forbearance?

"On the contrary, their principal business is to destroy each other. More than five millions of Christians are trained, educated, and drilled to murder their fellow-Christians. Every nation is groaning under a vast debt incurred in carrying on war against other Christians or defending themselves from Christian assault. The world is covered with forts to protect Christians from Christians; and every sea is covered with iron monsters ready to blow Christian brains into eternal froth. Millions upon millions are annually expended in the effort to construct still more deadly and terrible engines of death. Industry is crippled, honest toil is robbed, and even beggary is taxed to defray the expenses of Christian warfare. There must be some other way to reform this world. We have tried creed, and dogma, and fable, and they have failed; and they have failed in all the nations dead.

"The people perish for the lack of knowledge.

"Nothing but education, scientific education, can benefit mankind. We must find out the laws of nature and conform to them.

"We need free bodies and free minds, free labor and free thought, chainless hands and fetterless brains. Free labor will give us wealth. Free thought will give us truth.

"We need men with moral courage to speak and write their

real thoughts, and to stand by their convictions, even to the very death. We need have no fear of being too radical. The future will verify all grand and brave predictions.

"Science, the great Iconoclast, has been busy since 1809, and by the highway of Progress are the broken images of the past.

"On every hand the people advance. The vicar of God has been pushed from the throne of the Cæsars, and upon the roofs of the eternal city falls once more the shadow of the Eagle.

"All has been accomplished by the heroic few. The men of science have explored heaven and earth, and, with infinite patience, have furnished the facts. The brave thinkers have used them. The gloomy caverns of superstition have been transformed into temples of thought, and the demons of the past are the angels of to-day.

"Science took a handful of sand, constructed a telescope, and with it explored the starry depths of heaven. Science wrested from the gods their thunderbolts; and now the electric spark, freighted with thought and love, flashes under all the waves of the sea. Science took a tear from the cheek of unpaid labor, converted it into steam, created a giant that turns with tireless arm the countless wheels of toil."

How unfounded are the claims of the Church, that its religion has been one of beneficience, and that it has been the source of the advanced state of civilization that obtains in the world to-day! It has shed more blood in its own name than have all the other religions of the world combined, including Mohammedanism, which has been next to Christianity in cruelty. While the pagan religionists of the eastern world were pursuing the even tenor of their way, killing none because they did not believe as they did, Christians were saturating the earth with the blood of its children, and doing all in their power to force back the incentives to science, education, and a better civilization. The Christian rule, besides being a reign of bloodshed, terror, and the most cruel persecution, has been the most powerful impediment in the path of the progress of the human race. It has upheld the worst forms of superstition and error that the world has ever known. Its contest with growing science has been bloody and persistent. It has resorted to all its hellish arts and infernal inventions to throttle the comely young child of education, and to keep alive the grim and horrible monster of ignorance and blind faith. It has cherished, petted, fed, clothed, and made powerful the worst and most oppressive priesthood that has cursed the earth.

But its power is weakening. Its clutch at the throat of science is growing weaker year by year. A few more decades and its strength will become so exhausted, and its venom so far spent, that an era of light, knowledge, equality, and mental liberty may be ardently hoped for to reign on the earth.

As science gains supremacy over the myths and fables of superstition, persecution will more and more pass away. Men will be less disposed to torture each other and take each other's lives because their opinions cannot always exactly correspond. The more superstition and faith, the more persecution and bloodshed. The more science and demonstrated knowledge prevail among men, the more toleration and perfect freedom of opinion will abound. As supernaturalism retires to the rear and Rationalism and a belief in the laws of the universe advance and are looked to for guidance and wisdom, the more the happiness of our race will be secured, and the sooner will the enmity and cruel jealousies arising from diverging religious creeds cease to have an existence among the sons of men. Ignorance has been the great devil of the world, and science is its great savior. May it never more be crucified as have been the numerous fabled saviors of the past.

The conflict between religion and science, which, for two or three centuries, has been waxing more and more heated, is bound to continue until the weaker contestant is crushed to death. The enmity between them is irreconcilable, and no truce can be proclaimed that will have a lasting effect. The main contest must be between the Church of Rome on the one hand and Rationalism on the other. Protestantism is midway between the two, and must ultimately take sides with one or the other of the combatants. It cannot remain permanently where it is, and it is ardently to be hoped that the larger portion will step over on the side of science, reason, and truth.

In view of the irrepressible conflict alluded to, Prof. Draper uses this appropriate language: "As to the issue of the coming conflict, can any one doubt? Whatever is resting on fiction and fraud will be overthrown. Institutions that organize impostures and spread delusions must show what right they have to exist. Faith must render an account of herself to Reason. Mysteries must give place to facts. Religion must relinquish that imperious, that domineering position which she has so long maintained against science. There must be absolute freedom for thought. The ecclesiastic must learn to keep himself within the domain he has chosen, and cease to tyrannize over the philosopher, who, conscious of his own strength and the purity of his motives, will bear such interference no longer. What was written by Esdras, near the willow-fringed rivers of Babylon, more than twenty-three centuries ago, still holds good: 'As for truth, it endureth and is always strong: it liveth and conquereth for evermore.'"